GET BY
A survival guide for Black Gay Youth

Written by Jonathan W. Jones

LCCN 2005911156

This book is for two people: every Gay Black boy with hope in his eyes, and my mother - the most understanding woman to ever live. A special Thanks to both.

PREFACE

You should know that this entire book was written, not by a field expert, but instead by a real-life young Black Gay Man himself. I do not hold a Doctorate's degree in Africana Studies, or a Master's degree in human sexuality, nor a Bachelor's degree in child development. I have yet to conduct research for prominent institutions, or finish a thesis for an established graduate school. In fact, I hold only a high school diploma, and this book was written while I was in between my first and second year at Rutgers University. But although on paper I am presently no more than a mere "Freshmore", I am compelled to remind you that life – that is, the act of living – grants us no formal degrees. Life does not have consecutive grade levels, or standardized tests, or graduation ceremonies; only trial and error. The sole basis of this book is that I have, in essence, lived it; and the weight of my credibility lies on the shoulders only of what I have experienced.

However, instead of reading this book with a cynical attitude, keep in mind that my authenticity works to your advantage. Instead of reading a book published by distant professors - probably too old to render any idea of practical issues faced by today's Black Gay youth – you are gaining access to the advice of someone close enough to empathize with the many hardships you have had to endure. Instead of giving you a lecture-type rundown of the "do's and don'ts" of life, I am giving you candid conversation. And this, I feel, will best benefit you. This book is just one of the many resources an individual could use to enlighten himself upon the complexities of being Black and Gay. My method of conveying this message takes the more casual approach – similar to an older brother giving you sound advice that you can actually apply.

It is with this in mind that you heed my intent for this book, and furthermore, its impression on the text used throughout this publication. In writing this survival guide, I had to consider the variance of my audience. I wanted for Black Gay males ranging from ages 12 to 21 to be able to pick this book up and find it useful and understandable. Thus, I adjusted the vocabulary and language to be readable by a middle or high school student, while introducing them to new words that may be unfamiliar. I would hope that they would keep a dictionary nearby so that they can understand new words and expand their own vocabulary. Simultaneously, I tailored the language of the book to be comprehensible to the college man, while not seeming too juvenile.

Another deviation from the standard use of English in this book is my capitalization of the first letter in the word "Gay", to designate it a proper noun. The term "Black" earned its place as a proper noun to identify African-Americans in an honorable and politically correct way, and it is my belief that the GLBTQ community deserves this same rhetorical honor. I wanted the Black Gay male who is reading this to know that it is equally as significant to be Gay as it is to be Black.

It is with these actions that I hope to make this survival guide a book that can be used perpetually during the stages of life when the Black Gay man can be most unsure of himself. *Get By: A Survival Guide for Black Gay Youth* serves not only as my testament to climbing the great wall of adversity, but also as the hand I lend to help the next brother make it over.

Introduction

Why am I writing this book? So many people would ask me this question. But aside from the obvious dissenters in the outside "straight world" who have their own biased reasons for this book not being published, there were many within the Gay community who questioned this book's need to be created. There is already a bunch of books in the Gay market that talk about growing up Gay, they said. In fact there exists a virtual mountain of biographies, novels, films, videos, music, and more - all having to do with the tough process of coming into one's own sexuality as a Gay man. This is correct, I admitted. But then, I drew from a memory that I gained when I was the President of my university's Gay organization. My task was to compile a Gay media library for college students who were questioning their sexuality, or needed reaffirmation. I was to find a list of movies books, albums, etc, that would cater to the Gay individual – because it was important for us to see movies, read books, and listen to music that we could relate to. It was important that the characters in these art forms be Gay so that we understand that we have a meaningful existence in the world.

So I began with a search to fill up our video library. On a randomly-chosen video search engine, under the category "Gay & Lesbian", 27 pages with 16 movies each, returned – which is 432 movies that specialize in Gay cinema. Of course there are more Gay movies in existence than these, but I decided to start with this collection, because surely this list would contain the best, most popular movies among Gays and Lesbians. As I browsed through famous titles like "The Birdcage", "Wild Reeds", "In & Out", and "Billy Elliot", I suddenly realized that most (about 90%) of the people on the movie covers were White.

Therein lie the irony – I was given the task of finding people who I could relate to, people who looked like me, and was unable to find even one. These movies – supposed representations of American Gay life - had very few minorities in them. I thought, what if someone were to take these images as a depiction of the actual Gay community? Or worse, what if a young Gay person of color looked for affirmation and acceptance through media (often where youth turn for confidence) and is unable to find a role model or a respectable figure who resembles himself? What a tragedy this would be.

At looking at the larger society's perception of the Gay community, the image that comes to their mind when our name is mentioned is of a white Gay man. Much credit should be given to the white men, and women, who have fought valiantly to establish civil rights for Gays in this country: Harvey Milk, Elton John, Sir Ian McKellen. But the Gay community as a whole is comprised of more than just our Gay white male mascot. Our community is inclusive of women, bisexuals, transgenders, the intersexed, and minorities – all which have seldom been represented on the forefront of the civil rights struggle for Gay equality. The Gay Flag is a rainbow of six colors, expressive of how dynamic our community is.

When I was first trying to understand my homosexuality, my natural reaction was to identify what it was I was feeling internally. Always one to look for the answer in a book (I had a reputation as a nerd to uphold) the first place I went to for answers was the public library. And of the small archive they held on Gay culture, I remember that none of the pictures in the books looked like me at all, and for a while, I grew up thinking that in my small town of a black population, I was the only Gay person there. I was lost and had no place. And so, this returns me to the overall purpose for my writing this book: To let young Black Gay men know that, YES, YOU DO HAVE A PLACE.

<u>What You Are Up Against</u>

W ell, we all know that it's not easy being an African–American.
Of course, overt abuse has significantly declined since the days when our ancestors
were beaten merely for entering the wrong neighborhood, spit on for trying to
utilize the library, or lynched for winking at white women. But the psychological
oppression of the black man still exists today. Images in the media – many in our
own Hip-Hop culture – tell us that we are only capable of success through sports or
rapping. The number of black men entering colleges is declining while the number
of black men entering prison is rapidly increasing. The system of privileged white
men (not blaming, simply stating fact) has built a system in which we are constantly
struggling from the bottom to reach the top. This very system's upper levels are
relatively difficult to permeate with institutional racism against us, but the task of
upward mobility is doubly hard against those of us who happen to be born Black
and Gay. As if it weren't difficult enough to have people and system trying to
suppress us for racist motives, there exists many more who have, are, and will try to
knock us down because of sexual prejudices. And as if that weren't bad enough, the
two statuses often combat with each other. The black community is known for its
common anti-Gay sentiments, as there exists racism towards blacks from within the
Gay community. But there is hope! The key to surviving in a world with the odds
stacked against you from multiple angles lies in learning to balance the duality of
being both a strong Black man and a strong Gay man.

"So you're Black and Gay. Big deal," some may say. "In today's
world, the color of your skin doesn't matter, and neither does your sexuality. We're
all humans, so why does it matter. Can't we just all get along?" That's what a
person in an ideal society would say; that race and sexual orientation are nothing
but social constructs that mean nothing in how we are all treated. But unfortunately,
the world today has far from gotten over what country my ancestors came from, or
who I choose to seek companionship in. The truth is that my race and my sexuality
do matter, and so do yours. Our skin color/ethnicity and our feelings of desire
towards the same gender place us in a position in which we are labeled - and that's
natural. The first thing you see when you look at a woman is that she is a woman.
The first thing you notice when you see an Asian or Indian person is that they "look
Asian" or Indian. Society has to place people into categories in order to function
and maintain. And that is okay. Affirming that Barbara is a woman or that
Mohammed is of Arab decent is perfectly justifiable. The problem comes when
society associates people's characteristics with qualities that they THINK an
individual must have just because they are a member of a specific group. It becomes
a problem, for example, when we say Barbara is a woman, and because she is a
woman, she is weak. Or if we say Mohammed is Arabian, and because he is
Arabian, he wants to blow up the country.

These are stereotypes, and stereotypes lie behind people's prejudices,
acts of discrimination, and hatred of people from different cultures, genders,
religions, and sexual orientations. Concepts of what attributes accompany racial
identity are seen everywhere. When I tell you to think of a picture of a Black man,

what do you see? Most would probably see a tall, dark-skinned, muscular male. Just as when I say picture a Gay man, you most likely envision a short, soft-spoken, scrawny, androgynous figure. Peoples ideas of what it means to be Gay or Black cause them to see the two as immediate opposites – two identities that could not or should not be put together; and when they come across a Gay black man, their subconscious thinking becomes confused and the immediate reactions may be fear, disgust, fear, or hatred.

History Against Us

The legacy of oppression and a history of cultural stereotypes have placed a particular emphasis on notions of masculinity for black men. White slave masters beating our forefathers; white lynchers killing us for merely looking them in the eye; years of our community feeling that we have no power has emasculated us – stripped away our culture's manhood. And it is this conflict between Gayness and black machismo that encourages homophobia within the black community and goes back to the Black Power movement, which identified homosexuality as something weak and compliant and inspired by Europeans. The hard-core masculinity of hip-hop culture has reinforced those notions. What's more, African-American men historically have been denied access to the social establishment - and often have gained entrance based on physical demonstrations of strength or virility. For example, the pockets of rich black men (Shaquille O'Neal, Deon Sanders) who are only rich because of basketball, football, or some other sport in which the focus has been on physical capacity.

Machismo – that is the exaggerated sense of masculinity stressing attributes such as physical courage, virility, and aggression - has always been a strong component of the notion of black male identity. Therefore black men who have sex with other men are seen widely as antonyms to what it means to be a black man. Not only does this twisted concept cause the black community to hate the Gay man, but it works to cause the Black Gay man to hate himself. Black Gay men on "The Down Low" internalize this concept of "because I am Gay I am less of a man", and function in fear. They often times have wives and girlfriends, but simultaneously engage in sexual encounters with men – often without protection. This endangers both heterosexuals and homosexuals to the spread of infection, and more so, the spread of hurt emotions, secrecy, betrayal, and suspicion.

But I want to shift my focus off of Down Low brothers just to go back to the underlying cause of this unconscious self hatred: that the African American community as a whole is not accepting of its homosexual members. Black Lesbians and Black Gay Men are degraded, shunned, discriminated against, and oftentimes, physically abused. The homophobic pressures in Black schools, universities, nightclubs, churches, or Black culture in general.

Black Religion and Homophobia

In regards to homophobia in the black community, the focus of conversation has often shifted to understand Black Churches' stance on homosexuality. Many Black churches remain hostile places for non-heterosexual parishioners, and sermons regarding homosexuality often deem it as a practice comparable to murder, theft, and rape. We all know that most churches, whether Christian, Muslim, Jewish, or other, openly oppose homosexuality. But let me debunk the myth that the Black Church is the black community. The black community is not a bunch of people you can group together and say "This is their thought on the issue." Black people have always been politically diverse, with conservatives, liberals, radicals, and revolutionaries alike (and politics do not necessarily align with what religion you may identify as your own). But one of the major causes of anti-Gay sentiment within the African-American community comes from our reliance on religion. Historically, it was one of the only sources from which we could draw hope and perseverance. In the face of adversity; the master's whip, the lynch mob's torches, the policeman's brutality – we could also look skyward to gain a sense of purpose for continuing the struggle. Black culture and values are rich with Christian culture and values. It is with this in mind that, many unsure of what their thoughts on Gay people really are, turn to their "all-knowing Bible" and look for what the word says they should feel on homosexuality. They interpret the Bible to be anti-Gay and so they incest in these misconceptions and front anti-Gay beliefs themselves.

But, again, this is a problem in the African American community, because the Bible is interpreted in different ways by different people, and most often, people take what they want from the Bible and leave what they don't like behind. For instance, many teens say that the Bible proclaims says homosexuality is bad. The Bible also addresses the wrong doings in premarital sex, lying, cheating, stealing, respecting one's elders, and various rules emphasized by "the good book" but taken lightly. Another misconception is the belief that the Bible says homosexuality is (as one of my peers put it) "dirty, disgusting, and a sin." But the truth is that Jesus never spoke of homosexuality at all. Homosexuality wasn't even a word in any Bible before 1946. Anyone arguing that Genesis is "Adam and Eve, not Adam and Steve" is forgetting that the story is of the beginning of humanity. It's not a model for marriage or a way of living. And that's just what Christianity says about homosexuality. I must apologize, because I grew up in a Christian family, and am not totally familiar with Islam, or Judaism, so I cannot address specific contexts of homosexuality. But from what I understand, all religions protest an ultimate message of love and acceptance – not of hate and prejudice. All religions encourage the aid of fellow man, and no one can argue with that.

I readily admit, I don't know all of the reasons as to why the world contains a wide array of people who fail to accept and respect the Gay community, and moreover, why there is great tension within the Black community between its heterosexuals and their homosexual brothers and sisters. That Blacks people can foster hatred towards another minority group, especially after having the viewpoint of an oppressed group denied of human rights, is beyond my diagnosis. But the truth still remains: to be a Gay Black Man is a road in life that is both long and rigid. With a helpful road map (and the latest Diesel© shoes), each step can be as rewarding and exciting as the next.

Why Am I Gay?

What a question. "Why am I Gay?" This is a question that every Gay person has probably asked themselves, many throughout their entire lives. The question of where homosexuality comes from plagues both heterosexuals and homosexuals alike, and the continuing animosity towards Gays derives from their lack of understanding of where our feelings come from. You are most likely dying to know, too, why you are Gay. Why, while the rest of your male classmates are drooling after and chasing behind girls, you take an interest in the boys. Or what was happening inside of you that day you saw a gorgeous guy and, unexplainably, you felt a tingling, or a drop at the pit of your stomach. What is it that makes you aroused whenever you think of a man's round butt, creviced back, or smooth, sweaty abdomen?

Well, the truth is, nobody knows. There is no existing data that points to why some people like members of the opposite sex, and why some like members of the same. Some argue that it is an inborn trait, genetically passed on from parents to children. Others argue that is a result in the way that children are raised, that the environment influences sexual orientation. One study states that sexual orientation of a human being is determined within the first three years of their life, while the age at which lesbians, Gays, and bisexuals actually knew of their orientation ranged from 6 to 7-years-old to 40 or 50-years-old. Either way, there is no correct answer or theory that explains why we are the way we are. We just are.

The affirmation of our sexual orientation – that is firmly stating that we are Gay – also lies on an every-moving continuum. There are times when, for example, a Gay man may say he's Gay, and then over time, lose attraction to males, only to find after even more time, he is indeed attracted to males again. Conversely, there is a widely known surge of "heterosexual girls" who during adolescent engage in homosexual behaviors with other girls, but after years, claim that they have "grown out of it" and are now heterosexuals. Sexuality is a fluid entity of human life, and whether one is Gay, straight, bisexual, etc. is all based on what he or she identifies herself as. A man may have sex with other men frequently, but unless he submits to the label "Gay", we cannot deem him as a Gay man.

The fluidity of sexuality was best (in my opinion) researched by Alfred Kinsey.

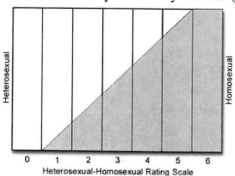

Heterosexual-Homosexual Rating Scale

Regarding homosexuality, Kinsey introduced the Kinsey Scale, which shows the variance of homosexuality, bisexuality, and heterosexuality in humans. The range from complete heterosexuality to bisexuality to complete homosexuality led to the notion that most people possess some degree of homosexual urges, but that they suppress these urges for whatever reason.

And so with that, I urge you to desert the endless search to find why you are Gay, but rather, to address the issue of societal separation between straights and Gays. You could spend an eternity trying to locate the gene that turns you on to boys, or you could fight a lifetime to make it okay for you and that boy to hold hands without being the target of hate.

 Black Gay History

The month of February is Black History Month. I've known this since the first time I had to make decorations in preschool of red, black, and green colored sheets of paper. I *just* learned that there is such a thing as Gay History Month. Yep, it's in October. Surprised that it's not on your calendar? I'm not. The recent Gay movement has caused a lot of clueless people to believe that "Gayness" is a fairly new thing – a fad, a new culture that arose out of people with common likes and interests; like Disco or Goth. But as long as people have inhabited the earth, I'd go as far to say that Gay people existed right along with them. And as long as Gay people existed….that's right, Black Gay people existed. Though Gay history is rarely documented, and even rarer Black Gay history, the truth is that you have a long history of identity that has made life as a homosexual minority more livable than the lives of men who came before him, and it's important to acknowledge those who have struggled for us to be where we are now.

The search for evidence of Black Gay History would be a daunting task, one that I personally am far from able to accomplish myself. Hence, I have simplified the process by procuring the great works of others who have taken on the genealogical job or archive-diving to find the remnants of the past so important to all of us. The Boston-based organization, The History Project, researched and compiled loads of data to give us this timeline of historical events relative to the Gay Black man of today:

Black & Gay History Timeline

1790 George Middleton, leader of The Bucks of America, an all-black Revolutionary War regiment, and Louis Clapion, a French mulatto hairdresser build and live together in the oldest standing house on Beacon Hill, at 5 Pinckney St.

1920 An artistic movement in New York that becomes known as the Harlem Renaissance establishes the reputation of Langston Hughes.

1926 Publication of "Smoke, Lilies, and Jade in Fire!!!" makes Richard Bruce Nugene the father of African American Gay male literature.

1938 Playland, Boston's oldest continually operating Gay bar, serves a more diverse clientele than any other bar in Boston. It closes in 1999 when the owner takes advantage of the skyrocketing property values in the neighborhood.

1938 The first issue of "Midtown Journal", a weekly South End scandal sheet, is published. Although not a Gay paper, it is the primary source of information for Gay men and lesbians about Gay life in Boston. The uniquely descriptive paper includes information about the working class, bohemian, and racially mixed South End neighborhood. The paper ceases publication in 1966.

1939 From October 1939 to April 1940 doctors at Worcester State Hospital administers experimental sex hormones to "treat" a black Gay man.

1950 The Napoleon Club, Boston's second oldest Gay club regularly features Sidney, an African American piano player and singer. His favorite song was Stranger in Paradise.

1950 Knights of the Clock, an interracial group of heterosexual and homosexual men and women, incorporates in Los Angeles.

1953 James Baldwin publishes his first novel, "Go Tell It On the Mountain". During the 60's Baldwin is a leading spokesman for the civil rights movement.

1963 Bayard Rustin, the prime architect of the 1963 March on Washington and aide to Martin Luther King, Jr. from 1955 to 1960, helps organize the Montgomery bus boycott in response to the refusal of Rosa Parks to ride in the back of the bus.

1966 The North American Conference of Homophile Organizations adopts the slogan "Gay is Good" after "Black is Beautiful."

1969	Rioting between patrons and police at the Stonewall Inn in Greenwich Village, NYC marks the unofficial beginning of the Gay civil rights movement.
1975	The first black men's group in New England forms in Boston. The Black Men's Caucus is organized to support non-white Gay and bisexual males "aiding the black Gay individual to assert his own identity and develop a sense of acceptance among Gay and bisexual men in the black community."
1978	National Coalition of Black Lesbians and Gay Men is formed.
1979	The First National Third World Lesbian and Gay Conference, organized by the National Coalition of Black Gays, is held during the first annual March on Washington in October.
1979	Mel King announces candidacy for Boston's mayoralty. He expresses commitment to the "entire diversity of the city -- and that includes Gays." The Gay Caucus for Mel King is formed.
1980	Boston branch of Black and White Men Together is founded to provide support to black men in interracial relationships. The organization is now called Men of All Colors Together.
1984	Black and White Men Together distribute "Boston Bar Study" a survey of discrimination in Boston's Gay bars.
1985	Breaking the Chains-Making the Link, sponsored by the Boston Rainbow Coalition, holds a meeting at the Harriet Tubman House to encourage solidarity among Third World and Gay activists.
1985	Dialogue, the second gathering of black, Asian, and Latino lesbian and Gay groups in Boston is held at the office of the League of Women for Community Service, a black women's service organization. The meeting is attended by members of El Comite, Black and White Men Together of Boston, the Black Men's Association, and the Lesbian/Gay Council of the Rainbow Coalition. The meeting lays the groundwork for future meetings and coalitions of people of color.
1985	The Lesbian and Gay Council of the Rainbow, Black and White Men Together, and El Comite co-sponsor a meeting with candidates running for the Boston City Council and School Committee.
1992	Ken Reeves, the first openly Gay African American City Council member, is elected mayor of Cambridge by his fellow City Councilors.

Source: www.historyproject.org

Everyone who ever stood for something has had a symbol that represents the meaning of their distinction. Symbols work both to emphasize our uniqueness (look at The Artist Formerly Known as Prince) and to band us together as one uniform identity. Here are a few symbols you may want to be aware of as a Black Gay Man.

 The African Flag – representative of Black people's ancestral roots in Africa, and of modern-day struggles against oppression of the African American community

 The GLBTQ (Gay, Lesbian, Bisexual, Transgender, Queer) Flag – the six colors symbolize the racial diversity of the GLBTQ community, and the notion that sexuality transcends ethnic, social, and economic divisions.

Pink Triangle – During the Holocaust, Gay men were imprisoned, tortured, and executed. To identify male homosexuals, concentration camp prisoners were made to wear the inverted pink triangle to mockingly signify their femininity. Currently, it is used as a positive way to note one's homosexuality.

 The Lambda -11th letter of the Greek alphabet, and the symbol for kinetic energy in physics. In 1970, The Gay Activists Alliance adopted the lambda to signify the energy of the Gay movement.

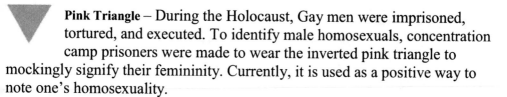 **Human Rights Campaign** – The symbol of a blue square with a yellow equal sign in it represents equality. This icon is used by the civil rights organization, The Human Rights Campaign, and one wearing it can be seen as a GLBTQ person, or one of our allies.
Transgender Symbol – This symbol, a combination of the male and female symbols, is used to identify those who feel they were born with the body of the gender opposite themselves (i.e., girl born with the body of a male, vice versa).

 Intersexed symbol – This figure represents those individuals born with genitalia and/or sexual characteristics of both or indeterminate genders. The word "hermaphrodite" has been used in the past, but has been since see as inaccurate.

Black Gay Role Models

Inspiration is a necessity for success. In order to strive to accomplish great things, people need a source of empowerment. One supply of encouragement comes from real-life people who inspire us to achieve: our teachers, our counselors, our mothers, or our neighbors. But as a Black Gay man, it will be helpful for you to envision your goals and know that they are attainable by learning from those who have experienced things from a point of view similar to you – a role model who knew the trials accompanying being black and Gay, but whose barriers were met by the faith in his conviction and the strength in his resolve. History has every so often presented us with Black Gay icons, who have blazed the trails we walk on today. These are just of few of such heroes:

Alvin Ailey - *Choreographer.* Founder of the world renowned Alvin Ailey dance troupe. Ailey combined African American movement with spirituals, jazz, and contemporary music in a unique fashion.

James Baldwin - *Writer and civil rights activist.* Baldwin was not afraid to speak out on issues of oppression. A prolific writer his works included: "Go Tell It On The Mountain", "Giovanni's Room", "Another Country", and "The Fire Next Time." An expatriate, Baldwin urged American society to discard its myths. He felt the most destructive myth was "white superiority."

Benjamin Banneker - mathematician, Washington, DC. As a clock that kept accurate also wrote essays on the

Mathematician. Self-taught astronomer and inventor who designed youth, Banneker invented a wooden time throughout his lifetime. Banneker evils of slavery.

Keith Boykin - *Attorney, writer.* Former Executive Director of the National Black Lesbian and Gay Leadership Forum. Author, "One More River To Cross". Formerly with the Clinton Administration as Director of Specialty Press. Boykin was present when Clinton met with Gay/lesbian leaders at the White House.

James Cleveland - *Clergy, gospel musician*. Cleveland founded the Cornerstone Baptist Church in Los Angeles and served as its pastor. He is better know for his work as a gospel recording artist, receiving a posthumous fourth Grammy for the LP "Having Church." Toward the end of his life he moved beyond internalized homophobia to become active in the fight against AIDS. He died of AIDS-related complications.

Langston Hughes - *Writer*. The writer most identified with the Harlem Renaissance. A prolific writer, he used almost every conceivable form to arrange his thoughts on paper: poems, songs, novels, plays, biographies, histories, and essays. His works include: "Not Without Laughter", "The Dream Keeper", and "Tambourines to Glory." He often said of his life, "There are some things I don't tell nobody, not even God. He might know about them, but it certainly ain't because I told him."

RuPaul - *Entertainer*. RuPaul Andre' Charles, six-foot-five black blonde drag queen who rose to the top of the dance charts as the "Supermodel of the World."

Bayard Rustin - *Civil Rights Activist*. Rustin was the chief organizer of the 1963 March on Washington. Civil rights leaders, concerned that Rustin's homosexuality and prison term as a conscientious objector during W.W.II might be used to discredit the march, asked A. Philip Randolph to be the march's official head. Randolph kept Rustin on as chief organizer.

These are but a few of the many Black Gay heroes that we have to look up too. I encourage you to do a little bit of research on your own to find out more about these individuals and the many more that exist. And hopefully, one day you will be one of the great Black Men who make a difference in the world and generations to come.

On "The Down Low" and in "The Closet"

The infamous closet. We all know what it is. When grandma hands you money for Christmas and says, "Don't spend it all on the girls", and you politely laugh and say "OK". When your classmate's telling you a dirty joke and asks your opinion about some girl he's hoping to "poke", and you simply agree and wait for the subject to change. Or those dreaded days in the locker room when you're really stiff (your movements, not your.....nasty) because you don't want to accidentally touch someone or get caught staring at something too long for fear of getting disastrously outed and beaten senseless by the jocks swarming around you. Being Gay surely isn't the easiest thing to be in the world, and in many cases, it's made that less easy when people know about it. Many Black Gay men find it easier to keep their homosexuality (or bisexuality) a secret – thus the term "Down Low" emerged to refer to men who secretly conduct sexual relationships with other men – or MSM's for short (**M**en who have **S**ex with **M**en).

Black men who lived double lives – one in which they portrayed themselves as faithful husband's to their wives, boyfriends to their girlfriends, and fathers to their children but secretly had sexual escapades with other Gay men – have probably existed for decades. But author J.L. King exposed this subculture in his tell-all book, "On the Down Low: A Journey into the Lives of 'Straight' Black Men Who Sleep with Men." His book offers astounding insight into why Black Gay men conceal their sexual desires. He admits that although he has sex with men, he doesn't refer to himself as "Gay" because he doesn't "want to get caught up in the whole Gay culture, because the media and people look at Gay people as being less than a man [in the black community]. The media has let white Gay people feel more comfortable in their skin and it's accepted. The greatest taboo is to be black and homosexual, and I refuse to be labeled and classified that folks will look at me as something different. I am a man."

His argument gives way to looking at the greater issue: the Black community's lingering homophobia. In the Black community, the label "Gay" carries a negative connotation, and for this, many young Black Gay men fear identifying themselves as such. Coming out has ended in people losing their friends, getting kicked out of the house, being cut off from parents' financial support, and worse. So although I cannot blame those who are dishonest about their sexuality, I have found that being out has been a gratifying experience. Whenever boys are curious about their sexuality, they often come to me to experiment. People who see that I am Gay and still generally cool and fun person, they come to dispel the negative beliefs and stereotypes about Gay people. This, in the long run, increases the number of people who understand and empathize with the plight of the Gay Black man, and these same allies offer there support voting on civil rights issues (i.e. same sex union legislation, anti-discrimination laws). Being an out Black Gay man is not always easy and it is not something I would suggest for everyone, but I definitely would recommend it to the strong at heart – he with a strong resolve who won't back down in the face of rising adversity.

Coming Out

Being out is not a fixed identify all the time. Some may be out to their friends, but they may hold the secret from their family members. Some may have told their mother, and left their father in the dark. Even some may have everyone in their town know they're Gay, but couldn't image proclaiming it on national TV! Environments change, as do the general attitudes towards homosexuality. Kissing a boy in the hallway is not the same as kissing him in church, and so we know that coming out – if you choose to do it- will be something you will have to do for the rest of your life. With each new town you move to, with each new job you get, or in any new situation, there lies a bundle of people who slowly must come to understand who you are as a person.

The Benefits

As mentioned before, confirming that indeed you are Gay will open up a load of potential partners for you. Initially, the already out boys will see you as "fresh meat" and be in a heated race to be the first to have you on their arms. And if that's not enough, soon you could become the Gay icon, the one who all the "straight but curious" boys hit on and look for to test their sexual curiosities. But besides that, being out provides a surge of relief. No more secrets swarming about how people think you might be Gay, no fears of someone finding out and blackmailing you. The pressure of having to pretend you like girls is gone. And overall, you can walk with a greater sense of confidence and self-assurance. Affirming that you are Gay can also hone your ability to defend your beliefs.

With all things, you've got to take the good with the bad. You may become the target of verbal, psychological, emotional, or physical abuse. So it is important that you weigh the pros and cons to your individual setting and conclude whether it is safe and realistic for you to out yourself. If you don't want to – or can't – proclaim your sexuality to others, that is OK. Do not feel pressured. Seeking advice from someone who is out or someone trained to help GLBTQ youth come out may be helpful. They can serve as a person to vent your emotions and lessen the feeling that you are alone with your feelings.

There are GLBTQ groups, counselors, teachers, your doctor, hotlines, and more – all aimed at helping the young Gay boy cope with the inner turmoil he may be facing. Access to the internet can help you find a wide array of people and services willing to help make your life that much easier.

How to Come Out

The first thing I would recommend before coming out is to know what the possible reactions will be. The best advice is to expect the unexpected, and then plan for it. The people you come out to may at first be in denial – naming all the reasons you can't possibly be Gay: "But, you had a girlfriend" or "it's just a phase you're going through". Some may be angry when you tell them, others disappointed, confused, or even feel guilty. "What did I do to deserve this?" they may ask. There are some who your sexuality would make no difference, and at times there will be those who say they already knew.

Each person's response will be different, and you can probably foresee how they will react by knowing what they feel about homosexuality in general. Indirectly ask them about their views on Gay issues in the news, or voice your opinions on an issue and evaluate their response. Keep in mind, though, that people's views on homosexuality often change once they know that someone they know is Gay.

Tips for Coming Out

1) Breathe
2) You don't have to say directly "I'm Gay!" You can say "I think I like boys" or "I don't think I'm straight"
3) Don't plan on doing anything for the rest of the night
4) Be prepared for a slew of questions about you being Gay
5) Sex is a hard topic for parents. Try not to use words like "fucked" or "sucked"
6) Naturally, hurtful things may be said to you. Try not to take them personally. Remember that they are surprised and that this is a natural defense mechanism.
7) Never come out during an argument or use it to hurt someone's feelings.
8) Know that they will warn you of how hard life is as a Gay Black Man is. Let them know that you were born Black and born Gay, and that you are strong enough to survive as both.
9) Counseling, church, or a whipping may be suggested as remedies for your sexuality. Let them know that these will not change you, but only make the relationship worse.
10) If you are coming out to your mother, you can persuade her with "You'll always be the most important woman in my life."
11) Have resources available for them to understand. (Video "Growing Up Gay" or PFLAG [Parents & Family of Lesbians and Gays] pamphlets).
12) Have resources for you to call as well.
13) Allow them time and space to think about the situation.
14) Always have a "Plan B". Set up an alternate place to stay if they kick you out, and money in case things get hectic.
15) Keep in mind that they may already know.
16) Be confident, and know that you've done nothing wrong for being Gay.

In any situation, there may be people who enlist in negative stereotypes and notions about Gay people. Lambda Institute compiled this list of some of the most common or frequently encountered inaccuracies people used in their generalizations about lesbians and Gay men in the early 80's. They were gathered from audience responses in workshops, seminars, and presentations. The myths and stereotypes listed are consistently held and do not seem to vary according to the age, sex, geographic location, or ethnic/cultural background of the person holding them. Here are some of the common Misconceptions and the answers you can use to combat and correct them.

Common myths and how to combat them:

Social Behavior Misconceptions

MYTH: Gay men act like women and lesbians act like men.

FACT: This is a common stereotype that is closely related to "all Gays look/act alike." The fact that some Gay men may act, appear, or actually be effeminate often makes them visible and recognizable as being Gay by the average non-Gay person. The obvious fallacy with this "recognition" is that not all effeminate men are Gay, and the actual number of Gay men who happen to be effeminate is a very small part of the overall Gay communities. The same dynamics apply to masculine women who are automatically "recognized" as being lesbians.

MYTH: Lesbians and Gay men are all "cross dressers."

FACT: This common stereotype is also based on the "all Gays look/alike" myth, as well as on the "Gay men act like women and lesbians act like men" myth. This stereotype confuses transvestitism (deriving sexual pleasure from dressing in the clothes of the opposite sex) with homosexuality. Studies have shown that 75% of transvestites are heterosexual men who enjoy dressing up in their wife's or girlfriend's clothes. This myth is often reinforced by the media when they seek out the most "sensational" images on which to focus in doing a story about Gay men or lesbians. There are also those people who identify as transsexual (their external gender does not match their internal gender). Most transsexuals are heterosexual; they wish to change their external gender and involve themselves with opposite sex partners. Unfortunately, the general public often believes homosexuals, transvestites, and transsexuals are all the same.

MYTH: Lesbians and Gay men are only found in big cities.

FACT: Lesbians and Gay men are members of society at large and are found in all geographic locations – from the biggest cities to the smallest towns and rural villages.

MYTH: Lesbians and Gay men like to "flaunt" their sexuality in public

FACT: What many people term "flaunting" with regard to lesbians and Gay men showing affection in public is simply seen as "cute" when non-Gay couples do the same thing. The basic difference is that we are so accustomed to seeing men and women holding hands, hugging, or giving affectionate little kisses in public that it almost becomes invisible to us. If we do notice, the usual reaction is "what a cute couple" or "it must be spring; love is in the air." But when we see two people of the same sex do the same things, we often have a negative or uncomfortable reaction. This happens because we are not accustomed to seeing it, and it is quite common for us to reject (at least at first glance) things that "stand out" as different or alien to us.

MYTH: Lesbians and Gay men are all liberals and radicals

FACT: Again, lesbians and Gay men are as diverse as society in general. There are Gay and lesbian Republicans, police officers, Mormons, lawyers, corporate executives, and so on. Of course, there are also those with less "conservative" occupations and affiliations.

MYTH: Lesbians and Gay men want "special rights."

FACT: This seems to be the new buzzword from the religious right. It is often coupled with the concept that Gay men and lesbians are not a legitimate minority since sexual orientation is a "choice." Remember that religious preference is also a "choice," yet it is given a great deal of protection from discrimination. Lesbians and Gay men are only trying to get equal protection under the law.

Sexual Misconceptions

MYTH: Homosexuality is unnatural.

FACT: When deciding what we are going to consider natural or abnormal, consider the facts. Homosexuality occurs in most mammals and birds. With respect to human beings, it has existed since the beginning of recorded history in all cultures and societies and among people of all ethnic, age, occupational, and socio-economic backgrounds. It accounts for at least 10% of the world population. With these facts, it is easier to see that lesbians and Gay men are no more unnatural than people with red hair (5% of the world population.)

MYTH: Homosexual acts are "strange" or very different from heterosexual sex.

FACT: What Gay men and lesbians do sexually is not much different from what most men and women do together sexually. When studies on human sexuality, sexual techniques, and styles of lovemaking are considered, it appears that heterosexual and homosexual sex have a great deal in common. In order to understand this, we need to think of the "whole picture" of sexual expression and gratification: sexual desire, emotional attraction, caring, love, attaining psychological and physical stimulation, all the forms of sexual foreplay, and the various ways of attaining orgasms. Then, with the single exception of vaginal/penile penetration, one can safely assume that anything a man and a woman
might do sexually together is probably the same or very similar to what two men or two women might do. Again, it is important to remember that not all heterosexual men and women have exactly the same sexual likes and dislikes or make love in the same way; the same is true for Gay men and lesbians.

MYTH: Homosexual sex causes AIDS and threatens society.

FACT: AIDS is believed to be caused by a virus, the Human Immunodeficiency Virus or HIV. As with other viruses, HIV can be sexually transmitted. It can also be transmitted through sharing needles when using intravenous drugs. AIDS is not highly contagious;

there is no evidence that AIDS can be transmitted through shaking hands, hugging, coughing, sneezing, insects, food, or toilet seats. You don't have to worry about working next to someone who has AIDS or sitting in a bus with someone who has AIDS or eating in "Gay" restaurants or shopping at 'Gay" stores. You simply don't get AIDS through casual contact! AIDS does affect a lot of Gay men; it is not however, a Gay infection. Lesbians are, in fact, among the groups at lowest risk. Heterosexuals are also at risk of HIV infection and should practice safe sex. For more information on AIDS, the U.S. Public Health Service has a toll-free hotline to answer questions. Call 800/342-AIDS.

MYTH: Lesbians and Gay men prey on children

FACT: Most child molestation involves male adults and female children. The media plays up male/male child molestation for many reasons; it is more unusual (and thus more newsworthy), it reinforces cultural stereotypes, it is more horrible since male children are more "valuable," and so on. The percentage of child molestation with female perpetrators is statistically insignificant. The secondary assumption with this is that you can be turned into a homosexual if you have a homosexual experience.

MYTH: Lesbians and Gay men play male/female roles during sex.

FACT: This is a very common stereotype. Its origin is probably in the "cultural conditioning" of perceived roles among non-Gay couples. Up until the early 1970s, American culture programmed us to believe that men and women had certain roles in society and in relationships. The common image was of the man as the aggressive, dominant "breadwinner" who worked to support the family and was the sole leader of the household. The woman was perceived as the passive "little woman" who stayed at home, kept the house clean, and served her husband. With these roles ingrained in us, it was common to try to put them on all relationships – whether they were heterosexual or homosexual. Thus, when people thought of two men or two women in a loving, lifelong relationship, they assumed one played "the man" and the other "the woman." With the contemporary trend toward equality for women in social, occupational, and family roles, along with the general equalizing of male/female relationships, it should become easier for people to recognize that lesbians and Gay men are not bound by the male/female roles of the '60s. Most homosexual relationships are based on a lifelong partnership of mutual sharing.

Family Misconceptions

MYTH: Lesbians and Gay men are not family oriented

FACT: Lesbians and Gay men are indeed members of families. They are mothers, fathers, sons, daughters, brothers, sisters, aunts, uncles, and cousins. Many Gay men and lesbians have extended families as well as the families or relatives of their spouses ... also known as lovers or domestic partners. They have the same range of needs and desires for family ties as non-Gays do.

MYTH: Lesbians and Gay men do not want to settle down with just one mate.

FACT: Here is another myth related to the "lesbians and Gay men are only looking for sex" stereotype. Many Gay men and lesbians have the same desires and needs as non-Gays to establish lasting, monogamous, one-on-one relationships with someone. Many Gay men and lesbians find such partners. As with non-Gay relationships, sometimes they last a lifetime and sometimes they end in separations. Possibly the only real difference between a Gay or lesbian "love" relationship and that of a non-Gay couple is in the area of legalized marriage. There is essentially no difference in the affectional ties, legitimacy, emotional ups and downs, fears, anxieties, commitments, or personal rewards.

MYTH: Lesbians and Gay men can't and don't want to have children.

FACT: Many lesbians and Gay men have the same drives to be parents as many non-Gays do. This fact is supported by the many support groups that exist for Gay fathers and lesbian mothers. Some lesbians and Gay men enter into heterosexual marriages in order to have and raise children. Others choose to adopt or to become foster parents. In addition, some lesbians use artificial insemination as a means for having children. Recent studies show that Gay men and lesbians are no more or less suited or qualified to be parents than non-Gays. When people learn that many lesbians and Gay men are parents, they often assume that the children will become homosexual. This assumption is not supported by scientific findings. On the contrary, a study in the June 1978 American Journal of Psychology reported that 36 out of 37 children raised by a sampling of homosexual parents were found to be heterosexual.

MYTH: Lesbians and Gay men can't "really" love their mates.

FACT: Gay men and lesbians are just as capable of falling in love and establishing rewarding and fulfilling relationships as are non-Gays

MYTH: Lesbians and Gay men are all atheists or anti-religious

FACT: Lesbians and Gay men are no less religious than non-Gays. Recent studies show that nearly every major religious sect has a Gay/lesbian following. This fact can be supported by looking at the number of Gay and lesbian churches and religious organizations.

Source: The Lambda Institute

Health

Go to any Gay Pride parade, glance through any Gay publication, or visit any Gay nightclub and it will come obvious to you how obsessed the Gay community is with the male figure. The boys with the cutest faces and the sexiest bodies are often heralded as gods among men, while those who sport and average or realistic image are often invisible. And so it is no wonder why it is suggested that Gay men are more at risk for body image disorders than straight men. Typically, Black Gay men probably suffer more teasing about their bodies when growing up, and may be more insecure about masculine gender identity, especially since body appearance is given higher value in both Black culture and Gay culture. Additionally, Black Gay men scrutinize (and are scrutinized by) other Gay men who may be potential sexual partners. They habitually compare their body with that of their partner, judging sexual attractiveness by who has less body fat, who has more musculature or who has the bigger dick.

Body image involves our perception, imagination, emotions, and physical sensations of and about our bodies. It's not fixed- but ever changing; sensitive to changes in mood, environment, and physical experience. You may look in the mirror one day and say "Damn! That boy is fine", and look in the mirror the next day and think, "Damn! What the hell happened to me?" The way we look is not based on fact. It is psychological in nature, and is influenced much more by personal self-esteem rather than by actual physical beauty as judged by others. The notion of how our body looks is not inborn, but is a concept learned by socialization - in the family and among peers - but these standards of beauty only reinforce what is learned and expected by the people we grow up around.

Know that it is natural for you to want to look good. There is absolutely nothing wrong with working out regularly, monitoring skin-care and acne, striving to eat a low-fat diet, or trying to maintain a healthy weight. Activities that improve body appearance are perfectly normal and reasonable if you want others to complement your inner beauty with your outer layer. But what is most necessary is for you to have a comfortable acceptance of your body.

Enhancing Your Male Body Image

* **Recognize** that bodies come in all different shapes and sizes. There is no one "right" body size. Your body is not, and should not, be exactly like anyone else's. Try to see your body as a facet of your uniqueness and individuality.

* **Focus** on the qualities in yourself that you like that are not related to appearance. Spend time developing these capacities rather than letting your appearance define your identity and your worth.

* **Look** critically at advertisements that push the "body building" message. Our culture emphasizes the V-shaped muscular body shape as the ideal for men. Magazines targeted at men tend to focus on articles and advertisements promoting weight lifting, body building or muscle toning. Do you know men who have muscular, athletic bodies but who are not happy? Are there dangers in spending too much time focusing on your body? Consider giving up your goal of achieving the "perfect" male body and work at accepting your body just the way it is.

* **Remember** that your body size, shape, or weight does not determine your worth as a person, or your identity as a man. In other words, you are not just your body. Expand your idea of "masculinity" to include qualities such as sensitivity, cooperation, caring, patience, having feelings, being artistic. Some men may be muscular and athletic, but these qualities in and of themselves do not make a person a "man."

* **Find** friends who are not overly concerned with weight or appearance.

* **Be assertive** with others who comment on your body. Let people know that comments on your physical appearance, either positive or negative, are not appreciated. Confront others who tease men about their bodies or who attack their masculinity by calling them names such as "sissy" or "wimp."

* **Demonstrate respect** for men who possess body types or who display personality traits that do not meet the cultural standard for masculinity; e.g., men who are slender, short, or overweight, Gay men, men who dress colorfully or who enjoy traditional "non-masculine" activities such as dancing, sewing or cooking.

* **Focus** on the ways in which your body serves you and enables you to participate fully in life. In other words, appreciate how your body functions rather than obsessing about its appearance. For example, appreciate that your arms enable you to hold someone you love, your thighs enable you to run, etc.

* **Aim** for lifestyle mastery, rather than mastery over your body, weight, or appearance. Lifestyle mastery has to do with developing your unique gifts and potential, expressing yourself, developing meaningful relationships, learning how to solve problems, establishing goals, and contributing to life. View exercise and balanced eating as aspects of your overall approach to a life that emphasizes self-care.

Drugs

Regardless of whether my mother will ever believe this, I have never done drugs. It wasn't luck that kept me away from them or hardcore governing by my parents that made me never want to experiment with illegal drugs. I just did. I know what drugs can do to a person, and I guess in fear of altering myself for the worse, I have always abstained from any drug use. But I would be naïve if I thought that most of my counterparts carried this same resolve about drug use. Movies, music, and television covertly glorify drug use, and the pressure as long as complacency of random drug use is everywhere in the Black community. And on top of that, the Gay party scene emphasizes pleasure, often associated with sex, but commonly associated with the use of drugs. So although, for the record, I'm telling you "Stay away from drugs; they're not worth it", I'm realistic in knowing that this will keep only about .0001% of my readers from experimenting or continuing with drug use.

Although I cannot persuade many from drugs, I can however enlighten them on responsibility with drug use. First off, drug use is illegal, so if you are going to do drugs, understand laws and consequences of being caught. Depending on where you live, you could spend 15 years in prison just for carry someone else's stash. Secondly, avoid using alcohol, tobacco, and/or drugs as a remedy for life's problem. They may help relieve stress momentarily, but remember that after the effects wear of the problem still exists. If you keep drinking, smoking, etc to get away, you'd actually just be digging yourself into a deeper hole. Thirdly, be aware of your actions and others with use. If you find yourself getting aggressive when intoxicated, chill, before you end up hurting yourself or someone else. If you need help with a drug problem, seek help. If a friend has a drug problem, help them with it. I always say that doing drugs is like playing with a loaded gun: if you're going to do it, make sure you "getcha safety on!"

ALCOHOL

<u>Other Names</u>: Liquor, "sizurp", cocktails, wine coolers, malt liquor, spirits, brew

<u>Effect of the drug</u>: Effects can occur within several minutes of ingestion, however the effects of alcohol are influenced by multiple factors relative to the user, including the user's weight, gender, tolerance level, whether food was consumed, and how quickly the alcohol was ingested:

• Feelings of relaxation or euphoria
• Reduced anxiety and/or reduced inhibitions

<u>Negative Effects/Overdose Effects</u>: Drinking alcohol to excess, drinking alcohol out in the hot sun, mixing different kinds of alcoholic beverages, or mixing alcohol with medications or illicit drugs accelerates the effects of alcohol on the body and can easily lead to an overdose. What is excessive to one drinker may not have much effect on another drinker and this is why drinkers must take responsibility for knowing their "limit". However, a drinker rarely realizes he or she has become intoxicated until it is too late.

<u>Excessive consumption of alcohol causes</u>:

- Loss of motor skills and lack of coordination
- Headaches
- Nausea
- Dehydration
- Muddled thinking
- Aggressiveness (in some users)
- Sedation ("passing out")
- Blood poisoning
- Coma
- Death

TOBACCO
Other Names: Cigarettes, cigars, pipes, chew, dip, smoke, butt, snuff, bone, coffin nail, cancer stick
Effect of the drug:
- Increased blood pressure/increased heartbeat
- Increased breathing/body temperature
- Euphoria
- Loss of appetite

Negative Effects/Overdose Effects:
- Increase in blood pressure, heart rate
- Increase of blood flow from the heart
- Narrowed arteries
- Chronic lung infection
- Coronary heart infection
- Stroke
- Cancer of the lungs, larynx, esophagus, mouth (smokeless tobacco, cigars)
- Cancer of the bladder, cervix, pancreas, kidneys
- Adverse birth outcomes in pregnant women

AMPHETAMINES
Other Names: Amphetamines: Uppers, black beauties, pep pills, crosses, hearts, speed.
Methamphetamines: crank, ice, crystal meth, rock, crystal, speed, poor man's cocaine.

Effect of the drug: The effects can last from approximately 4 to 12 hours, but the initial high or "peak" is gone within minutes of ingestion, leaving the user to face a "crash," or a low, desperate feeling which sparks a strong desire to use the drug again. The effects of smoking "Ice" can last up to 24 hours.
- Increased blood pressure/increased heartbeat
- Increased breathing/body temperature
- Euphoria
- Loss of appetite
- Feeling more alert and less tired
- Intense "rush" which only lasts for about a minute

Negative Effects/Overdose Effects:
- Irritability/anxiety
- Severe mood swings
- Overheating/fever

- Weight loss
- Difficulty sleeping
- Paranoia/hallucinations
- Depression
- Compulsive behavior, for example, feeling that there is something crawling under the skin. User will pick at the skin, or rub their arms over and over again.
- Nerve damage which causes symptoms similar to Parkinson's Infection
- Stroke
- Increased risk for AIDS/HIV or Hepatitis where needles are used
- Convulsions
- Meth psychosis/meth madness (similar to schizophrenia)
- Death

CANNABIS

Other Names: Marijuana, weed, bud, pot, grass, crippy, Thai stick, pillows (cannabis packaged in tiny baggies), reefer, Mary Jane, spliff, blunt, joint, roach, stick, ganja, hash

Effect of the drug: The effects of the drug are felt within ten to thirty minutes and may last several hours, depending on the amount used.

The effects include:
- Euphoria
- Mild hallucinations
- Increased relaxation
- Disorientation
- Increased appetite
- Lowered inhibitions

Negative Effects/Overdose Effects: In large doses, cannabis causes fatigue, "burnout," paranoia or psychosis. Long-term effects of cannabis use upon the body include cell abnormalities, impaired speech, loss of memory, lack of mental focus, inability to concentrate, mood swings, blurred vision, infertility, sinusitis, bronchitis or lung cancer, pregnancy complications and panic disorder. A breastfeeding mother can pass THC to her baby through breast milk.

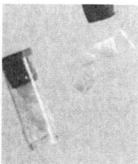

Powder cocaine   Vials of "crack" cocaine

COCAINE

Other Names: Cocaine: Powder, nose candy, blow, soft, snow, coke, base, hooter, "do a line" (inhale cocaine), Yeyo (Spanish), white horse, toot.

Crack Cocaine: Hard, freebase, baser, crack, rock, ball.

Effect of the drug: The effects from cocaine use are felt immediately and last one to two hours. Crack cocaine use provides a high that is incredibly potent, due to the way it is ingested. The effects of crack cocaine are felt almost instantly, quicker than any other drug. The "low" that follows this incredible "high" is what drives the user to seek another dose, or "hit" of crack cocaine. The effects of crack cocaine use last about fifteen minutes.

Effects include:
• Increased alertness, euphoria, and excitation
• Increased blood rate/pulse
• Insomnia
• Lack of appetite

Negative Effects/Overdose Effects:
• Agitation
• Hallucination
• Heart infection
• Brain seizures
• Mental illness (cocaine psychosis)
• Convulsions
• Death- Can result from a first time use if the user has significant health conditions, such as a heart problem. The dosage necessary to cause an overdose varies from person to person.

PCP (Phencyclidine)
Other Names: Phencyclidine- PCP, angel dust, rocket fuel, killer weed, embalming fluid, buttons, shrooms, mushroom tea, magic mushrooms
Effect of the drug: PCP: Effects are felt within 2 to 5 minutes depending on method of ingestion and may last up to 48 hours in some cases. Effects are similar to LSD including hallucinations, distortion of sensory perception, mood changes

Peyote:
• Mood changes
• Hallucinations
• Distortion of sensory perception

Psilocybin: Similar but less potent effect than LSD
• Hallucinations
• Distortion of sensory perception

Negative Effects/Overdose Effects:
PCP:
• Severe mood disorder
• Violent hostility (of special concern to Law Enforcement)
• Acute anxiety
• Drug-induced psychosis similar to schizophrenia
• Flashbacks
• Self-inflicted injury is common

Peyote:
• Difficulty distinguishing illusion from reality, "bad trip"
• Panic/anxiety

Psilocybin:
• "Bad trip"
• Panic/anxiety

Source: http://www.denisonia.com/police/Drug.htm

Again, although I want to make it absolutely clear that I AM NOT ADVOCATING DRUG USE, this is a survival guide, and my intentions lie in making sure that you stay safe under all circumstances. So it is with this in mind, that I present you with tips for staying safe and healthy in the even that you are going to be doing drugs.

If Doing Drugs.......

Make sure that you have food in your stomach and water in your body. Drug use takes vitamins from your body, so you must restore them with food and water before and after drug use.

Sleep is important, always. Staying up for extended periods of time may cause hallucinations and a weird itching feeling that resembles bugs crawling on your body. Even if you're on uppers, still rest your body periodically.

Chill in between dancing to allow yourself to breathe and rest your body.

If it's cold outside, wear a jacket. Just because you don't feel cold (or a coat doesn't match your outfit) doesn't mean your body will protect you.

Doing a lot of drugs simultaneously is extremely dangerous. Try to stay away from mixers and drug cocktails.

Drug dealers are naturally untrustworthy. Only buy drugs from reliable connections, like people you actually know or associates of friends.

Don't try new drugs if you are already on one.

Bring condoms...period. Being high is no reason to catch something.

Always remember it is against the law. So don't be loud or obvious about it.

Check for cuts, tears, or any raw spots on your body where blood. Semen or urine can enter.

Only do drugs with people you know and/or trust. When you are intoxicated, people may look to take advantage of you.

Being high may increase pleasure during having sex. But if you find tat you only enjoy sex with drugs, you may have a drug/sex problem. Talk to someone about it.

Be reasonable and responsible, about yourself, the people you are with, and the place you are in.

Relationships

Isn't it wonderful? When someone finally understands you and you understand them. You like him and he likes you, and as time goes by, the two of you only grow deeper and deeper in love. Yeah, that's the stuff. Most of us want it, or at least have wanted it at some time or another. Whether it's with a really good friend, a lover, or the man of our dreams, we all just want to feel connected to someone on, at least, and emotional level. Finding a person that takes interest in us comes easy to some. Others may need a little help. To start from any position, I would advise on have a home base, a support group known as friends. Friends – and I mean good friends – will help you on this venture as a Gay black man.

First off, we have to start with the obvious. It would be ideal for your friends to know that you are Gay. It will make telling all of the juicy details easier if you don't have to constantly remind yourself to turn all the "he"s in the story to "she"s. At first, I didn't have any Gay friends and the friends that I did tell shunned me when I told them I was Gay. But once I was outed (by a vicious rumor), the Gay boys flocked to be my friend. I wouldn't recommend outing yourself to the whole student body just to find friends – because you'll probably get just the opposite – but you should consider letting close people whom you trust in on your life. That way you can separate those who really are your friend no matter what, and those just blowing smoke.

Friends who have your back will come in handy when you need advice on an outfit, when you're too shy to approach the hotty who caught your eye, or when you're bored and can't find anything to do tonight. But more importantly, friends will be there when your heart is broken in two, when you come under attack by homophobic idiots, or when you think you have a serious issue that you're not ready to discuss with your parents yet. Finding a good friend to stand by your side is some of the best advice I can give you in surviving in, not only in Gay and Black societies, but in the larger world.

Most of this book has been oriented to males, but I definitely have to give props to the millions of ladies out there who serve in the divine position of "fag hag" – ultimate female best friend to the Gay man. A loyal woman makes an excellent accessory to man on the Gay scene. But whether you have one best friend, or a group of friends, setting up a support network is essential. The issue of male versus female friend is trivial. Females can connect with you on a social level that a lot of men naturally cannot. Male friends can discuss topics of sexual performance and things of that nature that women are biologically deficient in. It doesn't matter whether your friend(s) are male are female, and for me to tell you to prefer one over the other would be ridiculous. So I simply implore to find a good friend.

Groups of friends take different forms as well. The over-the-top (almost arrogant) Black Gay man is know to adopt an entourage – a faction of other men who travel with him and the group attends events together all the time. Some men hang with a group of gorgeous men in hopes that he will be seen as a gorgeous man too. The less handsome man hangs with a group of friends who look relatively unattractive to him, so as to make himself look that much better. Most groups like these are shallow and each member's concern for the other only rests in their collective ability to get attention. I would not advise camaraderie with people you do not truly like, but instead encourage for you to foster meaningful friendships. Truly great friends are indeed hard to find, but they are impossible to forget.

❧Dating❧

Dating - we see it every where. TV, movies, even music videos contain some element of meeting someone special, dating, and falling in love. I can't think of one film in which the main character didn't wind up kissing somebody by the end of the movie. Love is in the air, and to those of us who are Black and Gay, it may seem like all the people falling in love, getting married, and having babies don't look like us. There are but a handful of movies that have a homosexual of color as the hero. So what does this mean? We are free! Our minds don't have to follow the messages that mainstream media drown everyone else in.

A lot of the Gay culture's notions about how same-sex couples should perform have been based on the way in which heterosexual couples perform. Gays for a long time prescribed in the impression that even if it were two men or two women in a relationship, that one had to "be the man in the relationship" and the other be "the woman". Let me tell you firstly, that this is not only WRONG, but it is INSULTING. If one member of a couple naturally has more-effeminate qualities, and the other more-masculine qualities, then so be it. It happens. But how dare anyone tell someone else that they have to conform to the gender expectations imposed by a society that deems them deviant in the first place.

Oftentimes, we as Black Gay men confuse ourselves with issues of masculinity and sexuality. In the Black community alone, value is excessively placed on masculinity. In the Black Gay community however, the attribute of masculinity is widely ranked higher than a man's income-level, education, and appearance, combined. We look for a "real nigga" who we see as "a ganstsa" - but often has no money (or gets it illegally), no job, is an ex-con, is abusive, neglectful, and uneducated. Finding the right man is about finding the right person to complement you. Like a yin-yang, the two of you should use your skills, your emotions, and your understandings to create one unifying relationship. If you are a college-bound Black Gay man, you know you have no business with a man who's picture is hung up at the police station, because all it takes is for you to be in the wrong place at the wrong time and it results with you as an accessory to a crime, shattering all your dreams of a brighter future.

But, since I hear myself starting to sound like my ever-lecturing mother, I will end my sermon with these tips of advice when looking for the right one:

Make sure he likes you in your natural state: without the hazel contacts, the Prada outfit, the done hair, etc, etc.

He should respect your body & mind. Make sure he doesn't assume you're stupid or incompetent. And makes sure that it's not just about his pleasure, but yours too.

You should prescribe to what YOU like in a man, not what your friends/media think is cute. If you like guys who are slightly chubby, then stick to it.

Don't be shallow. All that glitters isn't gold, and that model-looking guy may actually be a real jerk.

One of the most attractive traits is modesty. So what if you look good? Nobody wants to hear you say it 24/7.

You are a Black Gay Prince – worth your weight in Platinum. So expect to be respected. And in turn, you should be respectful to him.

Once you have found someone who you see yourself in a relationship with, the key is to making the feeling of joy and excitement last as long as you can. When you feel that rush of energy every time he calls, and you can't help but smile the instant you two are reunited, that's what you have to make last. Taking this, and building upon it, is what makes relationships strong enough to stand the test of time.

One thing that Black Gay men have a lot of is ego. We can never be wrong, and we can never lose. Putting two people like that in a relationship has the potential to be divisive, but making it last is based on your willingness to concede from time to time. Admit that you may not be right all the time. If you are sure that he is wrong, let him continue until he sees his mistake. Or flip the situation so that he sees it from your point of view; so that he feels what you're feeling. If you two are compatible then you will be able to get along, but also realize and accept the things you do not have in common. That's what flexibility is – sometimes it's what you want, sometimes it's what he wants, and sometimes it's what you both want.

Important in relationships also, is honesty. Again, mind-games and ego may hinder your desire to be open with him, but know that a healthy dose of communication includes honesty. If something he is doing makes you jealous, tell him. Don't think that it will make you seem "whipped" or put him in control. If he really likes and respects you he will consider your feelings and react accordingly.

Independence and space are often immeasurable by how much is appropriate. You don't want to come off as his shadow, always right there with him, but you don't want it to be said that "you're never there". Give him private time and allow yourself some. Going away for a while will make it that much more exciting when you return.

Over time, people change – it's scientifically proven. So as you two change, spice things up a little to make things exciting a new all over again. Surprise him, experiment, be spontaneous, or try something new to add a little something extra to what you two have created together.

Don't be blind. You may be head-over-heels in love with him, but ask yourself if he feels the same as you do. Direct expressions of "I love you" may be said by each person, but sometimes "love" may not actually be the word to describe his feeling. Don't push the relationship too fast. It's common that one person feels a bit more intensely than the other, but make sure you don't force him to say things he doesn't mean. Conversely, don't let anyone push you to a point in a relationship that you haven't emotionally gotten yet. Not ready to meet his parents, or have him over for dinner? Let him know that although you do like him, you may not like him as much as he thinks you do. It's important to be clear that "I don't like you as much" DOES NOT mean "I don't like you at all." Make sure he knows that your feelings take time, and that he may need to slow up in order for you to become ready to move the relationship higher.

Out And About

Going out to a restaurant or to the movies is fun and exciting with someone you're really interested in. Infatuation is a beautiful thing, and yes a bit scary. You don't want to say the wrong thing, you don't want to come off as boring, and you don't want to eat something that makes your breath smell like a baby prostitute. But as if this weren't enough to worry about, you also have in the back of your mind that people will be offended by the fact that the person you're on a date with is the same gender as you.

If you and another boy are out and about, exchanging flirtatious glances, sitting intimately close to each other, or even kissing and holding hands, be prepared to be subjected to disapproving stares and comments from any direction. Virtually everyone - from young toddlers to the elderly - will be made aware that there are two budding homosexuals in the vicinity; as you should be aware that your survival could come into question at any moment. Of course there exists little pockets of heaven (The Village in NYC, The Castro in San Francisco) where you and your boy admirer could walk arm and arm and nobody even notice. But the rest of the world deems this a spectacle, and though times are changing, times are not yet fully changed. Public discrimination against Black Gay men is prevalent, and it is your duty to be aware of this and protect yourself and your loved ones.

Common Gay Places
If you or your beau are not out, or simply don't feel like being the object of torment, here are a few date places where you could go:

The movies - it's dark, and everyone's eyes are on the screen.

A museum – the artsy atmosphere is Gay-friendly and will allow you to explore each other's artistic likes/dislikes.

A walk through wooded parks – nice scenery and place where people go to just relax.

The mall – the mall is practically a "Gay haven" and you don't need money just to look.

A coffee shop – loungy atmosphere where everyone's chatting and minding their own business.

Bookstore – a large bookstore (Borders, Barnes & Noble) have secluded couch areas for talking and drinking cappuccinos, which is really sexy.

Take a long drive – getting away from the scene of your hometown or city can be exhilarating and romantic.

While You're On That Date

Maintain your composure and making sure you come across correctly will ensure that you snag the guy you've been trying to get There are certain Do's and Don'ts that you should keep in mind when out and on you date.

Do's	Don'ts
Make him feel comfortable.	Talk about yourself all night.
Keep the conversation going.	Be late.
Be an interesting date.	Talk too long about your ex.
Laugh at his jokes.	Eat with your mouth open.
Be on time.	Try to be something you are not.
Be yourself.	Disrespect him or his beliefs.
Talk about his interests.	Forget to thank him for the date.
Be romantic.	Pursue sex if he has said no.
Be confident.	Ask personal questions.

I Want ~~Somebody~~ Anybody!

There may come a time in your dating life when there is a **HUGE** gap between now and when you were last in a relationship. Don't fret. Being in a relationship isn't everything. If you find that you can't find someone to concentrate your love on, my advice would be to turn that love inward. Think less about finding the perfect mate, and think more about *being* the perfect mate.

I have long been an avid believer in continuous self-improvement. Whenever I was not in a relationship, I would focus all my energy on myself. I took longer baths, worked out harder at the gym, and ate healthier foods. Love yourself and others will love you the same. After a while, all that time at the gym sculpted my body to catch the eye of prospective dating candidates, and the longer baths and healthy diet made my skin smoother to the touch. So in the long run, not being in a relationship can benefit you if you use that time to your advantage.

How and Where to Find Him

Some unofficial survey has been cited saying that about 10% of all Americans are Gay or Lesbian. Even if we were to be generous and include into the equation that, let's say, half of that 10% is men, and half of those men are Black, we'd come up with the summation that only 2.5% of the US population is Black Gay men. 2.5% of the population (about 300,000,000) is 7,500,000. Divide that by 50 states and you get 150,000. So all of this seemingly pointless math will tell you that there must be approximately 150,000 Black Gay men in your state. Now take that 150,000 and assume about 25% of these men are 16-25 years of age and you come up with 37,500 eligible hotties within your state border.

My apologies for the annoying mathematics; the math geek in me is fighting to get out. But back to my argument, I came up with this number to show you that there are more than enough guys out there for you. "But where are they?" you may ask. Well that's easy. You just have to do a little searching – and that's the fun part. These 37,000 Black Gay men are not all waving rainbow flags and dancing the night away at your local Gay club. Some are closeted boys dancing with girls at the straight clubs. Some are hidden in small towns and home schools. Some of these number are Gay - they just don't know it yet!

That's where you come in. You have to strap on your private eye, and begin the hunt. If you go to a high school with 1,000 students, math says that around 100 of them have homosexual urges, thoughts, and/or behaviors. Most times, there are Gay guys in all the obvious places; the chorus, the drama club, the dance team. But, like my high school, you'd be surprised to know that many of the Gay boys at your school are in unexpected places, like ROTC or on the sports teams. Tennis is a dead giveaway, but look for hints on the football and basketball team of curious boys who give their teammates a sportsman's pat on the butt with a bit more enthusiasm than the others. My favorite sports games to go to in high school were swimming, wrestling, and basketball because if you didn't see any "potentials" on your school's team, you could do a little investigating with the players on the opposing team.

And school isn't the only possibility for meeting hotties. The internet hosts a slew of cute Gay guys (PLEASE TAKE CAUTION WHEN MEETING PEOPLE OVER THE INTERNET; THERE ARE A LOT OF "CRAZIES" OUT THERE!).You can go to a concert where Gay fans are sure to make an appearance. I say "behind every diva is a bunch of guys wanting to be just like her", and Beyonce is know to have a big Gay following. And if you see a cutie at an Usher concert and he's singing the words, you might as well wrap him up and take him home with you, because he is definitely "downe" (gay). Other hot spots for Gay/bi hotties are the mall, coffee shops, music stores, the library (surprised?), parades, among places with beautiful scenery, and anywhere where the sun serves as perfect lighting.

But the best part about Black Gay men is that we have the bravado to go anywhere everyone else goes. Some places are a little less Gay-friendly, and so we rely on our ability to assimilate into environments, which may make it more difficult in your search for Mr. Right. But if a cute Black Gay men catches your eye, and he wants you to know he's interested without telling the whole room "Hey! I'm a fag!", he will give off subtle hints that he's "one of us". Study these signals so that when the time comes, the chance to mingle with a fine Black brother does not pass you by.

The Signs

1) **The Stare**. If you see him and think he's cute, let him know that you're lookin' and you're likin'. If he's interested, he'll return the gaze, with a flirtatious gesture (maybe a slight eyebrow raise or a wink). Sometimes a turn away can be seen as "not interested, but can also be him playing hard-to-get. If he is interested, it will become an obvious game of back and forth eyeing, and if really intent, you two will become locked in a stare.

2) **The Smile**. If engaged in a stare, or back-and-forth eye glances with each other, smiling will secure the message that you two like what you see, and open the floor for one of you to make your move.

3) **The Body Flaunt**. In the wild, animals use their bodies to attract mates. And so this rings true to our species too. If he lifts his shirt, pretending to scratch his shirt, he really just wants you to check out his abs. Or if you arch your back or lean forward to display your…assets, then both gestures will be taken as non-verbal flirts.

4) **The Turn Around**. In the event that you are walking and someone coming your direction catches your eye, you can be sure that he is intrigued if, after you pass each other, he turns around to get another look. At this point you or he can either keep walking or stop and chat for a while. I recommend beginning the conversation with a compliment on what about him caught your eye.

5) **The Head Nod**. If a cutie has his eyes on you and he nods his head with a smile to sort of say, "How You Doin'?" Then understand that he definitely wants to know more.

6) **The Stalk**. Sounds a bit scary, but actually is kind of exciting. If you notice that he's walked pass your area a few times or that wherever you go, he seems to be there, he may be lightly trailing you, trying to get your attention. In the event that he's cute, just image that he's trying to think of something to say, and give him some time before you bring it to his attention. If you find him unattractive, nip it in the bud and let him know that his following you makes you uncomfortable. <u>In any event, be nice about it.</u>

7) **The Copycat**. A less predictable way for a cutie to get your attention would be by mimicking all you movements, sort of teasingly and playfully at the same time. He is looking to get your attention, but it may annoy you. To show him he has your attention, do an outrageously sexy gesture. If he does it back at you, it could make him your temporary puppet, and have him do anything you want him to.

8) **The Wingman**. This is where friends come in handy. If you're too shy to approach him – or to scared to face possible rejection – have your friend do the work for you. Your friend should go over there and point to your direction, while you look casually interested but not desperate. If it doesn't work, then oh well, he was ugly anyway. If it does work, be prepared to talk to him face to face with an interesting conversation.

♦ + ♦   Oh, the Possibilities   ♦ + ♦

A relationship means different things to different people. Even in the same relationship, each person has differing notions on how they should behave and what responsibilities they have in sustaining the relationship. A whole heap of drama is most often caused by people in a relationship not understanding what their expectations are, and failing to meet those expectations. In the wide, wide world of dating there are so many types of relationships that even I am amazed at how people can function together as one unit to foster and understand healthy emotions about themselves and the ones whom they care about. Here are the possibilities.

A Friend With Benefits: This is a friend with whom you share physical attraction to. He/she does not necessarily have to be a close friend, but just a friend who you like physically and are willing to have sex with recreationally. If you two are bored or are just randomly aroused, you can agree to have sex to pass the time, or get over boredom, sadness, frustration, etc.

A Jump Off: Someone who you do not regularly associate with, but you know that you can rather easily obtain sex from. Little to no emotion is involved in this relationship, and the sexual encounter is merely for short-lived pleasure. Physical attraction may not even exist at all, and conversation beyond what you want done sexually is limited.

A Boyfriend (Closed Relationship): There are two people in this relationship, you and him, who are exclusive to each other. This is the primary and only relationship that you can concentrate your emotions and sexuality on. You belong to him and he belongs to you, period.

A Boyfriend (Open Relationship): The open relationship takes many forms. One or both partners agree that it is acceptable to get sexually and/or romantically involved outside of the primary relationship. This agreement can be for one or both people. For instance, it may be half open, where it is OK for you to get involved outside of the primary relationship but not OK for him, or vice verse. Or there may be certain rules that you must follow when getting involved outside of the primary relationship, such as:

- If you have sex outside of the primary relationship, you must use a condom.

- If you get involved in outside relationships you will always remain true to your primary partner and never leave me for someone else.

- If you get involved outside of the relationship, you must tell me everything about it.

- If you get involved outside of the relationship, keep all evidence/information to yourself.

- To get involved outside of the relationship I must approve of the person or people you are getting involved with and/or approve of what you will be doing.

- If you get involved outside of this relationship, I must be a part of the experience too.

- Only sex is allowed, and you may not get emotionally involved.

The Triad: A relationship with three people. You have two boyfriends, who both know about each other, and are also dating each other. Emotions are shared with each, and a balance of interest is equally distributed throughout the three of you. If you buy something for one, you must bust the same for the other. If you have sex with one, you must have sex with the other. This relationship is very difficult to maintain because of jealousy, fear of favoritism, and inability to lessen your feelings for one boyfriend to match your feeling for the other boyfriend.

The Down Low: This is a secret relationship. Either you or he or both are not openly Gay, and so you keep this relationship a secret. The level of secrecy can vary among differing audiences. For instance, the Gay community may know that you two are dating, but straight friends and family may be totally unaware. Or the relationship may be so secret that only you and your partner know about it. Open acknowledgement and public displays of affection are forbidden.

The Circumstance Cheater: Like the Down Low this is a secret relationship, but it includes more than just you and him. This is the relationship with the "straight" boy who already has a girlfriend, and you are the "mistress". He lets you know that he likes you, but he's got a girl, and warns you not to get too emotionally involved. Commonly, when he is with his girlfriend, he may completely ignore you, or interact with you on a minimal level.

The Rebound: After a hard breakup, he is the guy who you cannot get emotionally involved in because you're still thinking about your ex. Dating him will warm you up to the possibility of jumping back onto the dating scene, but will ultimately leave him confused as to why he can't seem to get you to stop talking about your ex.

The Forlorn Lover: The guy who loves you; has a picture of you he kisses every night, but you have no feelings for. You feel guilty because it hurts you to see him hopelessly in love with someone who may never return the feeling. Be nice to him, please. We've all been there.

The Cyber Lover: He's the guy on your computer Buddylist who is perfect in every way, except that he lives a billion miles away. You met him online, you saw his picture, and he makes you smile with every touch of his keyboard. You wonder how much it costs to catch a plane to McFluggenville to see him just once. I say it's great to dream, but it's best to be real. Stop hugging the screen and go find you a real-life hottie. You can chat with him anytime.

The Jail Bait: He's the gorgeous boy who has a huge crush on you. The only problem is he's like half your age. Sure the age of consent is getting lower, and he looks like he's going to be even sexier when he grows up. But after a while, it gets weird when several people ask you if that's your little brother. Be friends, "adopt" him as your little brother, and show him how to grow up to be a respectable Black Gay man. Other than that, keep him away from Neverland Ranch.

Phone Hotline & Internet
<u>Dating Safety Tips</u>

We live in the information age. When we find that we can't happen to meet possible daters in person, we often resort to connections made through telephone and internet. Telephone chat line services and internet dating sites can connect you to people in your neighborhood, in your region, and all over the world for free. Meeting and dating people over the phone and/or the internet can be a wonderful experience, but in many cases, it has been used by vicious people, for very bad reasons such as stealing identities, preying on and stalking children, and worse. In order to ensure your safety and survival while utilizing the internet to find friends, dates, or more, I present you with these few, but important, phone chat and internet dating tips.

1.   Use common sense and exercise caution.

3.   Outline your intentions ahead of time. If you are only looking for friends, establish that. Whether you are looking for something platonic, or something a bit more sexual, let people know of what you are looking for to avoid misunderstandings in the future.

3.   Protect your identity. Don't use your real name or a familiar nickname. Make up a new anonymous nickname. Never include your last name, real email address, home address, phone number, place of work, or any other identifying information in your profile.

4.   Don't rush things. Do not become intimate (online or off) before you know the person very well.

5.   Be aware of odd behavior. Watch for warning signs such as bursts of anger, attempts to pressure you into things, if they seem controlling or overly aggressive, and if they avoid questions. If the person makes you uncomfortable in ANY way, do not hesitate to end contact and move on. Trust your "gut feeling". Do not worry about what they will think. They don't know you outside of your profile, so it doesn't matter.

6.   Record "facts" that the person tells you. This way you can look for inconsistencies. Pay special attention to their age, appearance, marital status, if they have children, and their interests / hobbies.

7.   If using the internet, ask for a photo. A picture is worth a thousand words. It's best to view several photos of the person in different settings to help you get a better idea of their personality, and what they look like from different angles. If they don't want to give you one, move on. If they agree, have them email it to you at an anonymous account that has no personal identifying information.

8.   You should be very comfortable with the person before revealing any personal contact information. Ask lots of questions and make sure you are happy with the answers.

9.   Using the telephone, use your ears to pick up more than what they are saying. You can learn a lot from a person's communication and social skill when you're on the phone.

10.   Only meet when YOU are ready. Telephone chat and online dating provides you with safe distance. When/if you fully trust the person, you can meet in person. Do not be pressured into meeting someone. If they truly cared about you, they would not pressure you. And remember, even if you did decide to meet the person, you have the right to change your mind.

11.   If meeting him, be sure to let someone know when, where and who you are meeting. Also let them know when you will be returning home. Try to carry a cell phone with you, and ask them to call you during your date to ensure everything is okay. When your date is over, call your friend or family member and let them know you are back from your date.

12.   Select a safe environment to meet in person. Do not go to their house or invite them to yours. Do not arrange for your date to pick you up or drive you home. Provide your own transportation. Meet in a familiar public place at a time when you're sure there will be lots of people around. Do not go anywhere secluded. Avoid hikes, walks, bike rides, and overnight excursions.

13. If you become uncomfortable at any moment during the date, do not hesitate to end it immediately. Be polite, and simply excuse yourself. If your date scares you in any way, don't second guess yourself – get out. Leave through a way where you are in sight of other people, or call a friend or family member to pick you. If you are really scared, call the police or talk to the manager of the place you are in. Explain the situation and ask them for help. Do not feel embarrassed. Your safety is most important – not how you look in front of a stranger.

14. Never give out your personal financial information. If they ask you for money, move on.

Making the Perfect Profile

Whether you are meeting people through telephone chat lines, or through the internet, first impressions make a big difference in how you come across to other people. You do not want to seem too piggish, too smutty, too arrogant, or too stupid to be dateable. You are like a package, and you should take it from a marketing perspective to highlight all of your good qualities to reel in that guy your heart is set on.

You definitely want to start off by being honest. Nothing is gained in the long run by portraying yourself to be something you are not. "Fakers" are eventually found out, and are oftentimes shunned by everyone when exposed. If you want someone who will like you for you, then be yourself, and avoid huge exaggerations or falsifying facts.

If you are using a telephone chat or you are not submitting a photo online, words are your best tools. A descriptive bio about yourself will best attract people who are lesser concerned with appearance in a picture, so you have to stimulate their mind with your language. Give a candid description of yourself, your interests and the type of person you are looking for.

Stereotypically but truthfully, Gay people have a tendency to boast arrogant attitudes. No matter how attractive one is, we all think that we are uniquely beautiful unlike everyone else. In profiles, it's only natural to brag about yourself. Just don't overdo it. Modesty also is attractive. The cutest guys are often the ones who act like the world doesn't revolve around them. Be cool in your profile, and make it about more than what you like and what you don't like in a man.

Include humor and wit in your profile. Make the person reading or listening to it laugh, as this will influence them to consider you as a potential partner. Most humor is acceptable, whether campy, cheesy, raunchy, etc; but do avoid racist, sexist, or prejudice-based jokes. A good profile makes the reader/listener feel like they can relate to you and urges them to want to talk to you more. Finish your profile on an inviting note.

Obviously, you shouldn't give out any personal information. Don't give too many details about where you live, where you go to school, places you hang out at, or even the names of friends that may rather go unmentioned. Your profile will be accessible by the billions of people on the internet or the hundreds of people on a phone chat, so only give out such information to people you've known for a while and have grown to trust.

If you are constructing an online profile and you decide to submit a photo, provide a recent, attractive picture of yourself. Naturally, people are more attracted to profiles with pictures than those without because a central part in choosing our mates is physical attraction. Sure it's a bit shallow, but blind dates can be hell. That's why a picture that presents you fashionably will work in your favor.

Outdated pictures send people a false image of you as younger. Pictures in which you look nothing like today will only deceived prospective suitors, so this should be avoided. Pictures of celebrities also can be harmful, as they create high expectations from the viewer. DO NOT take pictures of people that are not you and try to pass them off as your own. This is dishonorable, and makes you look very bad, as most people will assume that you are too ashamed of your real appearance to use your own image.

Your profile as a whole should make you seem attractive (not necessarily physically attractive) and approachable to the people who view/hear it. This is your time to do what most of us love doing: talking about ourselves. Give people a lasting impression, and the boys willing to entertain your desires will be lined up at your doorstep.

S...E...X

Mmm... "Sex". The chapter we've all been waiting for. But rather than start off with something juicy and scandalous, I'm going to tell you of a rather saddening event. Years ago, when my friend was telling me about the first sexual encounter he had with a boy, he confessed that afterward he ran to the shower to wash off the germs and "cleanse himself". He felt dirty. And as he scrubbed himself, nearly scratching the skin until blood was drawn, he stood and cried in the shower. He was naked and ashamed at the "highest sin" that he had just committed. Sure he had enjoyed himself physically, but he could not see past the feeling that this pleasure was wrong, and that he was now "damaged".

This boy *was* damaged. But not by the person he had sex with. He was done damage by the very people who taught him that sex was dirty. Countless numbers of adolescents grow up with distorted perceptions of what sex is and what sex means. The conservative majority is doing this nation's children a disservice by teaching teens to view sex as a dirty, unhealthy, and spiritually damning practice; and sex with members of the same sex a direct abomination. These unrealistic portrayals of sexual activity are not only inaccurate, but they are dangerous when accepted as truths by unknowing youth. Internalized anxiety towards sex can cause harmful sexual repression. When you couple this in with the stigma placed on homosexuality by the larger society, a child who has desires for members of the same sex is backed against the wall.

Insurmountable confusion causes the child to believe that his feelings, and therefore his being, is wrong, immoral, and unnatural; and these inner demons work to torment him in his every waking moment. As if puberty alone didn't present children with enough difficulty in understanding the workings of the body, the young boy whose wet dream is about his best friend, or who in the locker room gets frequent unexplainable erections – has the odds stacked against him. Natural reactions to his feeling of helplessness may be separating himself from others, depression, expressing his rage through violent acts on property, others, or himself, and thoughts of suicide.

Conservatives contest against the educating of children on sexuality with the argument that it will lead to a perverted culture with widespread rape, teen pregnancy, and loss of morality. But the true "loss of morality" lies in stripping our youth of the ability to understand how their bodies work in full. Sex is a natural thing, as is homosexuality. Educating adolescents on sexual exploration - while exercising safety, self-respect, and morality when doing it - will in turn breed a culture that is not afraid to appreciate and embrace the human form in its entirety. Sex is good. It is not just a form of procreation, but it is a form of concentration on the ones we love and look to understand on a higher level.

And yes, sex can be a fulfilling experience for many people, but sex is not for everyone. I want to stress that in a society that seems to place so much emphasis on the importance of sex, that to not have sex can be just as fulfilling. Just because it may seem like everyone else is going off somewhere and "doing it" doesn't mean that you should feel pressured to do anything that you are unsure or uncomfortable about. Abstinence has many benefits. You avoid sex-related drama, you don't have to worry that someone is interested in you for sex only, and it is the only mode of complete protection from catching sexually transmitted infections. Whatever you chose to do – have sex or not – know that your decision is based entirely on what you believe is best for you.

So with that said, let's get it on!

How many ways are there to tie a knot? How many ways can you make a S'mores? So many that you can't count them on two hands. The same with sex. There are so many ways and formulas in which two (or more; or less) people can create pleasure out of stimulating the human body. It's always fun to have one sure way you know you can "get off". But my best advice it to try new and different things every so often. When you become dynamic in your sexuality, you will find that you pleasure yourself in all kinds of ways, and in addition, learn to see yourself in all new manners.

To start off, I will begin this guide with who your first concern should be about: you! If you are going to be having sex, you need to know how to have sex with, well, yourself. That's right. I'm talking about masturbation – choking the chicken, spanking the monkey, or petting the one-eyed snake. Whatever you want to call it, it is what it is – exploring what parts of your body become aroused and what it takes to stimulate them.

Starting from "Square One", you may have noticed that whenever you see, feel, or hear something arousing – be it parts of someone's body, pictures, a sexy voice, etc. – your penis becomes longer and harder. As you masturbate, you will probably think of or envision sexual images. These images allow you to discover what it is that turns you on and what your sexual desires are. Do not feel guilty or ashamed of any desire that you may have, as they are important to shaping who you are as a whole person.

At arousal, the body of the penis and the head become more sensitive to the touch. Masturbation is most often when a person holds the penis with one hand and jerks it up and down – like milking the udders of a cow. When greater stimulated, the Cowper's gland secretes a fluid commonly call "pre-cum". Pre-cum is variant by the person – some people create a lot of it, while some notice very little or none at all. Pre-cum is simply a transition lubricant that comes out when the penis is stimulated. After prolonged and heightened stimulation, one will reach orgasm – which is marked by a tensing of the muscles in your body and nerves in the pelvic region contracting. Orgasm is accompanied by ejaculation which is when semen, commonly called "cum" comes out of the tip of the penis. Orgasm creates a tingling sensation throughout the entire body and after such climax one may find that he is tired from the "workout".

Get Wet!

The penis is stimulated by touch, so the more smooth the touch the better it will feel. The friction of the hand and on the penis alone can create sweat, which makes the up-and-down movement more pleasurable. But in the event that you want to reduce the traction and make the feeling even better, you gotta get wet. Here are a few lubricants that will heighten your penis pleasure:

Spit – "Yuck!" some may say. It seems unsanitary and barbaric, but when you're in a bind you may have to improvise.

Pre-cum – If there's enough in supply, then pre-cum adds a perfect coat to your polish job. The only drawback is that pre-cum has the potential to carry STIs. Be careful when using with partners.

Soap – If the escapades begin in water, soap can add a little slickness to the situation at hand. No pun intended.

Vaseline – Petroleum-based lubricants like Vaseline or gel are thick, but still work if you need to get greased up. Be wary though, things can get messy and clean up can be difficult. NEVER USE WITH CONDOMS!

Baby Oil – Oh yeah, Black people have been using baby oil with sex since Shaft was on the scene. (A guy named "Shaft"? Hmm). A personal favorite that adds shine to the body, making sculpted abs, pecs, and round butts glisten. Caution should be taken with fabrics though, because it stains. NEVER USE WITH CONDOMS!

Water-based Lubricants – Examples are KY Jelly, Astroglide, and Wet. Probably the most recommended for safety, easy clean-up, and wetness, water-based lubes do the same as the others but throws in versatility. Water-based lubes are the only lubes safely used with a condom.

If you've uhh…. mastered masturbation with yourself, feel free to add another person to the equation. Having someone else masturbate you, or masturbating alongside someone can be a way for you to let someone else explore what turns you on. If someone else is masturbating you and you feel his style isn't working, don't be shy to correct him delicately and instruct him on what it takes to get you off. Not everyone's technique is the same. The key to arousing different people is through learning and adapting to each person's style.

Where Your Mouth Is

Your mouth is an entry way to your pleasures. Why do you think they say the way to a man's heart is through his stomach? It's because the mouth has the ability to combine our senses of taste and touch to create a sensation that surpasses the feelings we get from most of the other organs on our body. With another person, expressing your love for him can be done by kissing him, nibbling on his ear, hickeys, or oral sex. The mouth can perform a lot of things, and is important in sharing emotions with your man.

Kissing

Black Gay men are probably the best kissers in the world, in my opinion. Our Black heritage has equipped us with a set of lips designed especially for smooching, and as Gay men, we know how intimate the mouth can be. Kissing your boy can be the perfect way to remind him how you feel. And there is seldom a time when a kiss is inappropriate. You can kiss him when he is leaving, when you're on the beach at sunset, in the morning, after a long time apart, at the movies, by moonlight, by candlelight, and practically anywhere or anytime you want to feel that buzz. As long as there is passion behind that kiss, you will leave him breathless. Here are a few tips on what you should keep in mind in order to make your kiss unforgettable.

First off, to be a good kisser you have to relax. Don't over think the kiss. Just be confident and assured that it takes nothing for you to show your man how much he means to you.

Ensure yourself that your breath is desirable. Gum or candy is suitable although not always necessary. Some candy/gum can heighten the kiss if the taste is erotic and satisfying.

Some people like it when you kiss with your eyes open, but the majority find it creepy. Close your eyes to allow your other senses to become sharper. If you are uncomfortable closing your eyes all the way, draw them down to where you can peak through them.

Begin your kiss with your lips either just slightly parted or closed. No tongue. Do not go zooming in at him with a huge slobbering tongue! You're giving him a kiss, not a mouthwash.

Loosen up your lips, and as they touch his, draw your mouth open so that your tongue meets his. Slightly tilting your head so that you can create a seal around your mouth and his would be good.

Move your tongue in a caressing motion, like you're licking at ice cream, teasing his tongue with yours. Every so often, close your mouth slightly then open it back again to allow your tongues to meet.

Breathe through your nose between closing and opening your mouth. DO NOT blow gusts of wind into his mouth. That is not cool or sexy in any way at all. If you think you are going to laugh, close your mouth and end the kiss.

Don't forget that you have hands. You can slightly touch his back, arms, shoulders, neck, or head. Or you can fully embrace him. Boys who like aggression may like it when you playfully pull them into you and kiss them.

To shake things up periodically, you can kiss them on other places than the lips. You can lightly kiss them across the forehead, include small kisses in between the big ones, or bite or suck gently on their upper or bottom lip.

The Infamous Hickey

Ever see someone with a mysterious darkened area on their neck that wasn't there before? It could be that somebody simply hit them in the neck with a baseball, but the odds are that somebody hit them in a totally different way. The "hickey" – the infamous love marks that everybody gossips about, is what happens when someone intimately sucks on your neck. What actually is happening is that the person sucking on your neck is pulling the skin, causing tiny blood vessels beneath the skin to break. These broken vessels cause a bruise, but the scar is painless, and it's nothing but a mark of evidence that someone has had their mouth on your neck. The act of getting a hickey, or giving one, is romantic (however hard that may be to believe). You and the person are engaged in a form of foreplay, and allowing someone to kiss, toy with, and suck on your neck, can be very arousing. You doing the same to your boy will leave him – and everybody else – talking about your expertise in the sensual department.

Giving a hickey is simple. As if you're kissing him, place your lips on the side of his neck around underneath where his jaw begins. Open your mouth into a circular formation – as if you were saying the letter "O". Lick the neck, with mouth closed, as if it were ice cream while you suck his skin into your mouth. Don't be afraid to get aggressive, as this is what creates the excitement he will feel. Avoid use of the teeth. After a while the bruises will form and "Voila!" you just gave him a hickey.

Suck It!

"Oh no he didn't!" Yes. I did go there. Brace yourself, because I am about to begin my lesson on oral sex. The art of fellatio is often viewed by outsiders as a submissive act. "Suck my dick!" is a common slur used against women to demean them. But that derives from the larger society's misguided comprehension of sex itself. Sex in the straight society is used to dominate one gender over the other and turn sex into a struggle between the powerful and the powerless. Fortunately, we in the Black Gay community are well informed of the balance in sex, and we know that to "suck dick" is by far one of the most exciting and liberating experiences one can ever do.

It allows you to see the male tool at its strongest and watch it at it's most fragile. You are given the chance to witness its satisfaction, and feel it pulsating through your body. Oral sex can be the most erotic of all engagements, and to master the ability to "give head" is to make yourself capable of rendering your boy's heart defenseless against your seduction.

Whether people call it "giving head" "sucking dick" a "blowjob" or what have you, the technical term for oral sex performed on a man is "fellatio". To give fellatio, and pretty much be a member of the Black Gay Man's Club, you have to love your boy's penis. Do not be afraid to touch it, or look at it. Don't hold it away from you at arms length, or only touch it with gloves on. The penis is a beautiful thing, and you must love it. Each one is different – big, small, straight, curved, long and short. In order to perform GOOD oral sex, you have to appreciate the beauty of a dick.

The best way to understand how to perform oral sex is to have it performed on you, so you know what is done and how one goes about doing it. If you think your partner performs exceptionally well, then tell him, and ask him what he did. This compliment will lessen the pressure that he feels, make him feel comfortable with you, and persuade him to give you some pointers on how you can perform just as well as he did. The experience of receiving a blowjob is intense, so in order to give, you should first get.

Oral sex is widely called "sucking dick" because, well, that's what it is. Simple right? We'll see. To perform oral sex, you should first open your mouth to let the penis in. Once inside your mouth, close your lips, BUT NOT YOUR TEETH, over the penis. Using just your tongue, lips, and the walls of your mouth, suck on his member and move your mouth up and down along the shaft and head of his penis. Try to create a simple up and down rhythm that you keep consistent. Once you set this rhythm, your partner may follow with thrusts of his penis to create that gliding sensation.

If your partner begins to thrust his penis too deeply into your mouth, you may become anxious, fearing you may choke. Stay calm and control this by using your hands to regulate how far he can go into your mouth. You can either place your hand at the base of his shaft and push his pelvis back whenever he pushes too deep, or you can fist your hand around his penis and move your mouth only to where your hand is. The use of hands is important during oral sex. Use your hand to apply adequate pressure to the shaft and the base of the penis. Or use your hand as an extension of your mouth, using it to jerk the skin of his penis in rhythm with your mouth. With your free hand you can cup his butt, massage his chest or legs, or whatever you feel will turn you or him on.

Cuming, Dear

All great things must come to an end. The best things usually go out with a "Bang!" and so, the best and final part of your sexual adventure will be his ejaculation. Many boys are particular about when, where, and on what their partner ejaculates. What can I say; semen is a sticky topic. With oral sex, you have the option for him to pull his penis out before he ejaculates, or he can keep his penis in your mouth as he "nuts". If he stays in you, you can either spit it out afterward, or swallow it. Do you know which one is safer? Swallowing is safer because spitting may bring the fluid into contact with possible cuts in your mouth. If the semen is infected with an STI, you could become infected too. But I am by no means advocating for you to swallow cum if you are uncomfortable. The safest means is to avoid any ejaculate from entering the mouth altogether. Whatever you choose should best accommodate you, and your partner should be made aware in advance so that you don't end up with any unexpected surprises.

__Hittin' It__

In the media, anal sex is what separates the Gays from the Straights. Sodomy is what they call it, and they try to compare it to all kinds of heinous acts. But the truth is that anal sex is just another way for two people to let each other know that they are happy to be together. In fact, there are surveys that show that anal sex is not the most predominant sexual activity among Gay men. There are many Black Gay people who never have anal sex, and there are some who find it scary and painful. I would remind you that you should never feel pressured into having any kind of sex. Your body is your concern and you should have final say in what you take part in and what you choose to avoid.

With that said, know that anal sex can be as wonderful an experience as any, with the right person. For some it takes time to do it comfortably, and for others it is non-stop pleasure since the first time. You have to be ready for anal sex emotionally and physically. If you feel that this is a task that you are ready to take on, here are a few ways in which you can prepare yourself.

Receiving:

Taking a penis up the butt may seem as simple as bending over and taking it in, but believe me, it isn't. Black Gay men in pornos seem to take dick like they have pussies. But in reality, being the receiving partner in anal sex (also known as being the BOTTOM) can be a lot more challenging. Straight people will ask, "doesn't that hurt?" And to be honest with you, for the bulk of Gay Black men, yes it does hurt – at least the first time. To take it in you, you have to be prepared for something to insert your anus. Prior to receiving someone inside you, you should practice by yourself with CLEAN fingers, dildos, or other personal objects. Relax your muscles and become used to the feeling of having something in there. Eventually, you will build up a tolerance, which will turn into a feeling of stimulation and arousal.

Once you've become accustomed to penetration on yourself, then you can allow someone else to endeavor. Starting out, the most comfortable position may be on your side, where you can best relax your entire body. Remind them to enter slowly at first, as you relax your muscles to permit entry. Pain is not unusual, but it will subside after a while, and you and your partner will feel joy together. Don't hesitate to stop if the pain becomes unbearable. His penis may be pushing too roughly against the walls of your anus. Recommend changing positions or taking a break to give you a period to settle and relax.

Anal sex is most erotic when the Bottom has a clean colon. Whether one's butt is clean is often a concern for both partners during anal sex. An appearance of feces during anal sex can be embarrassing, and may cause hygiene suspicion and/or gossip saying that the bottom gives "shitty deals" – slang meaning that that a person has anal sex with an unclean colon. You can prevent this from happening by assuring that your anus is clean at all times. Bathe or shower daily, paying close attention to your rectum, and wash immediately before any anticipated sexual encounters.

A douche – usually used for vaginal hygiene – can be used to clean out any stray particles of waste. The douche is a finger-like tube attached to a bottle of cleanser, which is inserted into the anus and releases a cleaning agent. The cleaning agent works to collect waste and you then defecate the remaining waste particles into the toilet and wipe your anus clean. The douche has dual benefits in that it hygienically prepares you for anal sex and it familiarizes you with the feeling of penetration ahead of time. Douches can probably be bought anywhere toothbrushes are sold (supermarkets, pharmacies, dollar stores).

The use of lubrication and condoms will put both your butt and your mind at ease. Latex or Urethane condoms will increase the amount of safety involved in intercourse, and decrease any anxiety you or he have about transmitting STIs. Anal lubrication will do wonders for lowering the amount of pain you feel, and the lessened friction will make his enjoyment even greater.

One of the most important roles of a Bottom is to keep your rectum as healthy as possible. Bowel movements should occur regularly. Constipation and diarrhea lead to other anal problems such as hemorrhoids, skin irritation, and anal fissures. These all can cause fecal matter to make an unwanted appearance during anal intercourse. Drinking water and including foods high in fiber in your diet will encourage a healthy and regular rectum.

Giving:

If you are going to be engaging in anal sex, and you are going to be the partner penetrating the anus (known as being the TOP), there are certain things you have to consider before willy-nilly sticking your dick into him. The first thing you need to understand is that this experience may be painful at first for the Bottom. So you need to begin slowly. There is a fine line between pain and pleasure during anal sex, and so your partner may be enjoying himself one moment, and in pain during the next. Pay attention to his expressions. If his "Oh, Yes"s turn into "Oww"'s then be ready to slow the speed on your joy riding.

Don't be sloppy. Any man can stick his penis in something and "get off". Make it fun for the bottom by creating a rhythm. Thrusts should create a pattern that the Bottom can pick up and adjust his anus to contract as you go in and out of him. Also along the lines of his pleasure is your consideration of how he feels. In the male anus, there exist a prostate that can be stimulated. If you are inside of him and you see his pleasure increase when you make a certain move, repeat that move. If you milk his prostate enough, he will reach climax along with you.

Proper lubrication is very, very, very important in anal sex. As a Top, it will often be your job to apply the lubrication. Make sure that your penis and his rectum both have enough lubricant to make for a lasting smooth ride. If, after some time, you feel things drying up, apply a little more. To avoid the hassle of pausing, pulling out, and re-inserting, my advice to you would be to keep the lubricant nearby.

A Top should also be knowledgeable of different sexual positions. In the event that your Bottom is uncomfortable, you should be ready to accommodate him and change to a more desirable position of continued bliss. Here are some positions that may help:

- **Doggie Style** - The Bottom kneel or stands bent over and the Top approaches from the rear.
- **Missionary** - The Bottom is on his back with legs open and knees near his head. The Top lays on top, facing the Bottom, and inserts.
- **Anal Drop** - The Top is laying face-up and the Bottom sits on his penis.
- **Side Anal** - The Bottom lies on his side and the Top, on his side also, approaches from the rear.
- **Lying Down** – The Bottom lays on his stomach and the Top approaches from the rear on top of him.
- **Wheel Barrel** - The Top approaches the Bottom from the rear, like Doggie Style, but lifts the Bottom's legs into the air. The Bottom must support himself by extending his arms on the bed, floor, or chair.

Versatile:

My theory is that the best Bottom knows what it is to be a Top, and the best Top knows how it feels to be a Bottom. I would urge for anyone trying one position to try the other. That way you have an understanding of what your partner feels when he plays the role opposite of you. Those who refrain from being exclusively Top or Bottom are referred to as Versatile – because they are interchangeable, and able to perform any sexual role you throw at them.

One thing that I cannot stress enough is the use of condoms. We as Black Gay men are rapidly contracting HIV and dying, all because we feel that "it feels better without a condom". If the condom is uncomfortable, my tip would be to buy slightly bigger sizes. Even a large female condom used during anal sex provides more protection than no condom at all. Protection is protection, no matter what. Shield him and shield yourself – wrap that rascal up!

S.T.I.'s

"Don't ride your bike without a helmet" mom always used to say. But who actually rides with a helmet on? It's not cool, and it looks funny. Plus it takes all the fun out of riding - with that big old ridiculous thing on me. This is often the same sentiment towards condom usage in the Black Gay community. When asking partners of mine to strap on a condom before we engage in sexual activity, I've been met with all types of excuses - from "it's too small" to "I don't like the color". And then there's the notorious "but don't you trust me?" bit. The Black Gay community has one of the highest rates of STI infection in the world, and it's in part by our own refusal to protect ourselves.

I bet if I were to get into a bicycle accident, from the day afterward, I would never ride without a helmet again. It's just a tragedy that sometimes it takes the same process to happen for people to learn that STIs can be prevented by condom usage. Sadly, I often find that it's not until someone catches an infection, that they realize the importance of safe sex. Fortunately for some, the first STI that it takes for them to "wise up" is nonfatal and curable – a strain of Chlamydia, a case of gonorrhea, or something that clears up after 7 days with the help of a pill. But the worse cases have put themselves at risk and contracted an infection that will follow them for the rest of their life – or worse, strips them of life entirely. This cycle of infection in our community, though, can be fought with knowledge. As a Black Gay Youth, you need to know what dangers lie out there, and what you can do to survive against them.

	SYMPTOMS	TREATMENT	PREVENTION
Chlamydia	• Often nothing, until the Chlamydia spreads. • Pain or stinging when pissing. • Discharge from penis or anus. • Inflamed and painful anus. • Sometimes affects eyes and throat.	Chlamydia can be successfully treated with the use of antibiotics	Using condoms will reduce the risk of infection.
Genital Warts	• Pink lumps, varying in size on penis, scrotum (the sac holding testicles), or anus. • Can become fleshy cauliflower-like lumps.	A special liquid is painted on to the warts. They can also be frozen off. Early treatment is advised.	Warts are caused by a virus. The best way to prevent infection is to avoid direct contact with them. Using condoms will reduce the risk of infection.
Gonorrhea	• Pus-like discharge from the penis and/or anus can be yellowy green. • Pain when pissing or shitting. • Sore throat. • Possibly no symptoms until it spreads further.	It can be completely cured with antibiotics.	Gonorrhea is a germ which can be passed on through sexual contact, anal and oral. Using condoms will reduce the risk of infection.

Hepatitis B	• Often nothing - but can be detected by a blood test. • Sometimes flu-like symptoms. • Tiredness. • Jaundice - yellowish skin and eyes, and urine can be dark.	A serious liver infection, which can make you very ill. Hepatitis B can take months to recover from and in some cases can be fatal.	Hepatitis B is the only STI that can be prevented by vaccination. The virus is mainly passed on through sexual contact. It is infectious and is present in blood, feces, saliva, and semen.
Herpes	• Small painful blisters (cold sores) around the mouth and genital area. • Discharge from the anus. • Pain when pissing. • Irritation on the lips, anus and genitals. • Flu-like symptoms as the infection spreads.	Tablets and cream can reduce painful irritation and treat further outbreaks. Herpes cannot be cured as the virus never leaves the body but outbreaks can be suppressed.	Herpes is a virus passed on through sexual contact, anal and oral. You should not have sexual contact until the sores have healed. Using condoms will reduce the risk of infection.
HIV	• Often none. People can stay fit and well for many years, and not know that they have HIV. • Symptoms can differ from person to person and may occur several years after infection. These can include night sweats, swollen lymph glands, and recurrent infections.	There is no cure for HIV, the virus that leads to AIDS. Once you have the virus you remain infectious for life.	Anal sex without a condom carries a very high risk of infection, using a condom will reduce this risk.
NSU (Nonspecific Urethritis)	• Sometimes no symptoms at all. • Abnormal discharge from penis or anus. • Inflammation around the genital area. • Desire to piss more frequently. • Pain or burning when pissing. • Flu-like symptoms	Antibiotics can treat most NSU infections. When no specific treatment is available, the doctor will prescribe something to ease the discomfort. If left untreated NSU may lead to inflammation of the testicles and be extremely painful during sex.	NSU is passed on during anal and oral sex. Using condoms will reduce the risk of infection.
Pubic Lice	• Itching in the genital area. • Check for small crab-like parasites and eggs in pubic and body hair if itching is experienced.	Crabs can be treated with special lotions. The instructions with the lotions should be followed carefully. Do not use just soap and water.	Crabs can be easily passed on through close contact, not necessarily sexual. People who have had close contact should check themselves
Syphilis	• Sometimes none at all, but can be detected by a blood test. • Painless sores on the penis, mouth, or anus. • Rash on the body. • Flu-like symptoms.	If treated early Syphilis can be completely cured with a course of antibiotics. If left untreated Syphilis can cause mental illness, blindness, heart infection, or even death.	Syphilis is present in blood and other body fluids and can be passed on through contact with these. Using condoms will reduce the risk of infection.

Source: http://www.gmhp.demon.co.uk/health/STI/index.html

SAFER SEX

Communication is the key to any good relationship. If you want your boy to know something, you have to let him know it. Whether communication is by outright verbal expression, hand gestures, or hints, you can always convey a message to him; and if he's listening, he'll pick up on it and respect what you're saying. And so, this should hold true with conveying the very important message of having safe sex. If you absolutely want to use a condom, tell him. And if he refuses, tell him again. Here are some ways in which you can remind your partner about the duty you have to protect yourself.

Whenever the topic of sex comes up, let him know that you only have sex with condoms. If he asks you, are you a Top or a Bottom, you may answer and then say "and I always use condoms". Most guys will accept this, but be prepared for the ignoramus who objects with strong reasons as to why you think it is necessary to use them. Do not let him argue with you and try to persuade you into doing something that questions your safety.

Before sex, hand him a condom. The message will be obvious and he will know that you intend to use it. Also you can put a condom on him and/or have him do the same to you. You can sexually put on a condom using your mouth if you place it on the tip and roll the sides down using your lips. The experienced Bottom can also place a condom on the tip of a penis and sit on the penis to roll the condom over it.

Keep condoms in a place where you and your partner can easily access them in the heat of the moment. A nightstand near the bed, on the floor near the bed, or under the bed may work to ease the routine of reaching for a condom into you two's sexual habit.

If during sex the condom breaks, stop and get another condom. If you are all out of condoms, then don't risk your health for one night of passion. You could end up regretting it for the rest of your life.

SiZe

Does the size of a man's penis really matter? Uhmm........Yes! I know, I know. It shouldn't matter, but you've got to face the facts. As a man who is both Black and Gay, your penis size will be the topic of countless discussions. The Black community already places emphasis on the supposed superiority of the Black man's sexual size and stamina. And as if that weren't enough, the Gay community places even greater weight on the male body, specifically the penis. So, thanks to the numerous myths and generalizations built up over the years on both sides, the Black Gay men is held in high regard when it comes to how large his member is and how well he can "work it".

Look at the porn industry, which objectifies Black men to the extreme. Adult entertainment advertisements of "Big Black Cocks", "Thugs With Big Dicks" and "Black on White Gangbangs" all hollowly glorify Black men as sexual beings. Even the popular phrase "once you go Black, you'll never go back" has done the Black Gay male damage in his dating relationships with other races. The countless white men who happily say that they want a Black *man* often really mean that they only want a Black *dick*. And when they get that Black man, and he's not rough, or uneducated, or ghetto, or well-endowed, he's as good as dead to them. (It's funny how White men will always enjoy a "hung nigger," huh?)

But it works to wage war against the Black Gay community the same. I could write on and on about the psychological damage done to us by placing value on the size of a man's penis, but who has a big dick and isn't proud of it? Despite that penis size has nothing to do with sexual satisfaction or manliness, I can't help but love big dicks. They look nice, they're fun to play with, and they seem to taste a little extra sweet! But with that said, I also need to look at the not-so-large penises in the community (metaphorically) and embrace them as well. Inclusion of everybody is the message I'm trying to get across.

I know too many "size queens" who will love a Black Gay men for the sole purpose of having a huge dick. A man could be abusive, polygamous, deceitful, and manipulative, but if he's holding weight in his pants the size queen would subject himself to his torment just for that fact. This is ridiculous! I have never been a fan of discrimination of any sort, and so one must understand why I do not feel compelled to watch the cultural tyranny on penis size. I must advocate for us, as a community, to value the differences within our entire Black Gay brotherhood. The dick is not the only big organ one can be blessed with. The brother who may not have a big penis, may instead have a big brain, or instead may have a big heart. Cherish him, and all he has to offer.

And while we're on the topic of size, let me discuss the debate over "cut" and "uncut". Whether a man is circumcised or not has the tendency to carry connotation in the Black Gay Community. Often, those who are "cut" believe that penises with foreskin are "dirty", "funny looking" or "weird", while those who are "uncut" think that the circumcised penis has a decreased sense of pleasure, are not intact, and are generally smaller than "uncut penises". We know that these are all lies; and to let such things as trivial as these cause friction among us is juvenile. I implore all Black Gay men to simply open their minds to see beyond what ignorant cultures have forced us to value. In doing this you will find that the part of your man that fits best with you is his love.

Deeper...:

Into the Ball Culture

You may have never heard of it, or maybe you have. Maybe you're knee-deep in it. Whatever the case may be, there is always something to learn about "the Ballroom Scene". The Ball culture is a world that is so complex, that to describe such a thing to someone who is unfamiliar with it becomes heralding. It is a subculture, with standards and values, and an existence that is unknown by many. It is an underground community that celebrates the individual talents possessed by Black Gay Men that go unnoticed to mainstream society.

To best explain what the ball culture is, I would have to ask you to simply open your mind to envision such a thing. Imagine that you are in a dance hall, at night. The large room is filled with Black and Latino Gay men – some dressed as women, mostly  everyone in extravagant or fashionable attire. Chairs are set for an audience, chatter and music are amidst and then, the program begins. An emcee introduces – along with the judges and other noteworthy attendees - the people who are hosting this Ball. They are an organization of Black Gay men ranging in age, known as a "House". This House resembles a large fraternity of all Black Gay Men, and the heads are referred to as the "Mother" and "Father" of that House. This hosting House is not the only House there. The entire ball consists of people from different Houses who represent their organization in tonight's venue. The Ball itself is marked with the night's theme, which seems to be in conjunction with the costumes and attire that the people there are wearing.

You see in the middle of the room, a designated space, called a "runway" which is where contestants from the Houses will compete, also called "walk". The competitions are divided into categories and each House submits its best contestant(s) for that category. Submitted contestants then "walk" against opposing House members to earn the recognition of winning that category, or defend the title of reigning champion in that category. A panel of judges critiques the contestants of each category, and names the winner. As the program progresses, winners of each category are presented with trophies, and the evening finishes with a Grand Prize category, usually offering cash and a trophy to the winner.

Essential to this culture is the dance form known as "vogue". This form of dance, an apparent combination of martial arts, modern dance, and gymnastics, encompasses flamboyant body movements that stay in tune with the beat of the music. Each move accentuates the baselines, rhythms, sound effects, and vocals of the music playing in the background. Voguing is based off of high fashion poses - like those seen in the popular fashion publication, "Vogue" magazine. Black Gay Men, a long time element in the fashion industry, have taken the act of posing for a camera and merged it with the art of dance. While voguing, the dancer enacts each pose rapidly in conjunction with the beat, which is meant to mimic the fast-clicking camera of a fashion photographer.

Competitive voguing seems to be the main attraction at Balls. The high energy of the Ball seems to pour into the vogue dancers engaged in a battle. Each one attempts to perform a movement that is flashier than the other, and the dancer himself gains confidence from the audience's approval. Dancing has always been a part of African–American culture, just as it has been prevalent in Gay culture. Voguing is the Black Gay man's incorporation of both lifestyles into a performative way of venting the anger, fear, and frustration that goes on inside every Black Gay man.

In Black Gay culture's context, this is what a "Ball" is. Jenny Livingston's documentary "Paris Is Burning" details the history and relevance of the Ball Culture. A tradition since the early 1900s, Houses get together every so often to collaborate on throwing a Ball to provide predominantly Black Gay youth with an outlet that highlights their interests and talents. The Ball culture, although close-knit and almost insulated – at least from the larger white community - is very accepting to the interested Black Gay youth.

The Ball culture is complex – comprised of its own rules, terminology, and networks. But once entry is gained, one can find a whole host of people that readily identify and support him. The basic unit of the Ball Culture is the House. The leaders of a house are referred to as the Mother and Father, although both may be male. Membership is granted by the Mother and Father, to eager kids who often have been rejected by their families, schools, churches, and their community as a whole. House Mothers are commonly seen as the role model; as they mentor, watch over, and provide for the young Black Gay men whom they are trying to readily prepare to face the harsh realities of oppression and desertion.

The size of a House can vary from having but a group of local members to having a huge national constituency. And not all the House's members "walk" categories. Some are enlisted to aid members with the preparation of an event or contestant. Honor is gained through showmanship and/or longevity, as members work to reach the ultimate status, know as "Legend" or "Icon". To become a Legend or Icon is somewhat like being inducted into a Hall of Fame. Those in the culture will uphold your reputation as one of the greatest contributors to the community of Black Gay men in the Ballroom Scene.

The only huge point of debate lies in that the majority of participants on the Ball scene possess relatively feminine traits. Black Gay boys and men who are "cunt" – the word used to describe a man who acts femininely – have built and sustained the Ball Culture. Those Black Gay men who shun, and more specifically reject, any celebration of feminine qualities in men tend to find the Ball culture undesirable. Masculine men and/or men who only seek friendship or companionship with "straight-acting" Gay men may find the Ballroom scene repulsive and will avoid any interaction or attendance with such a group.

(My Thoughts on the Ball Culture)

On many levels, there exists a divide between masculine men and feminine in the Black Gay community; and this is most visibly seen between those involved in the Ball culture and those who denounce it. Many masculine Black Gay men condemn "acting Gay" and believe that Balls are the epitome of what it means to be "too Gay". While conversely, a common category at Balls is "Boy Realness" - a competition in which feminine males impersonate masculine boys in attempt to convince the audience that they are a "real" boy. The use of the word "real" touches on two perceptions: (1) the Black community's belief that a "real man" is masculine, and (2) the world community's notion that a "real man" is straight. Are feminine boys not real boys? Are masculine men still not real if they are Gay? I say that Black Gay men as a whole need to "be real" with themselves and throw out the larger society's way of defining what a "real man" is. We are whatever we strive to be, and as long as we know that we have to be all that we can be, we will define for ourselves what it is to be a Black Gay man.

Say What?
Ball Scene Terminology

Inside of the Ballroom Scene, there are certain things you should know and certain words you should understand – that is, if you want to survive. Here are a few of the words you will find used amongst those who are in "the know" in the Ball Culture:

Amazon – *(noun)* the division of tall contestants within a category; without regard to gender.

Banjy - *(adjective)* the street-savvy look.

Battle - *(noun)* a tie breaker; the chance for a contestant to upstage his opponent.

Big Boy/ Big Girl - *(noun)* a class of ball competitors, usually 250 lbs. and over; "Luscious" may be used instead to refer to females.

Bring (It) – *(verb)* to challenge.

Butch – (noun*)* a masculine female, usually lesbian.

Butch Queen - *(noun)* a Gay male, ranging from "straight acting" to flamboyant.

BQ (Butch Queen) in Drag – *(noun)* a Gay male in women's clothes that is not taking hormones to become a woman.

Chants - *(noun)* clever rhymes and raps used by the emcee to liven up a competition.

Chop - *(verb)* to disqualify (a contestant).

Come (for) - *(verb)* to challenge, or attempt to humiliate; *"Don't come for me, 'cause you don't want it..."*

Craft(ed) – *(verb/adjective)* to steal/stolen or obtained by illegal means; "That purse was crafted".

Cunt(y) - *(adjective)* highly feminine.

Father/Mother - *(noun)* a house leader (without regard to gender).

Feel (it) -*(verb* to be ecstatic or joyous; to feel good.

Grand March - *(noun)* the opening ceremonies. The hosting House's members are introduced, along with the categories they represent. Mother and Father are introduced last for maximum effect.

God(dess) - *(noun)* the title given to the current or consistent winner of a particular category.

House - *(noun)* a social group of predominantly Black Gay men involved in the Ballroom scene.

Icon - *(noun)* a ballroom history maker; beyond the status of a Legend.

Judy - *(noun)* a close friend.

Legend(ary) - *(noun/adjective)* a multi-trophy winner, with a ballroom history; a veteran.

Live - *(verb)* {rhymes with "give"} to enjoy oneself greatly; *"I lived at that last ball!"*

Midget - *(noun)* the division of petite or short contestants within a category; anyone shorter than male/female model industry standards.

Ovah - *(adjective)* variation of "over"; meaning either "very impressive", or "disgusting".

Pay (it) - *(verb)* to ignore and move on; *"Pay it. I have other things to worry about."*

Prince(ss) - *(noun)* House son or daughter most likely to take the lead as mother or father should the current parents not continue their role; "heir to the throne".

Punish - *(verb)* to greatly surpass (competitors) in performance.

Read - *(verb)* to insult someone by highlighting their flaws and verbally exposing them.

Ruler - *(noun)* someone currently known for winning a particular category.

Seed(y) - *(noun/adjective)* an undesirable person, or described as such; low rated

Shade (throwing) - *(verb)* underhanded dealings, showing a spiteful attitude; *"He won't say hi to me; he's throwing shade".*

Snatch - *(verb)* to win.

Star - *(noun)* a potential Legend; a frequent winner who is making a name for themselves.

Statement - *(noun)* a potential Star; not always winning, but frequently winning.

Turn (it) - *(verb)* to make a grand showing; to be very impressive to the audience.

Virgin -*(noun)* a first-timer who has never walked (a particular category) ever.

Walk - *(noun)* to enter a category.

Source: http://www.balls.houseofenigma.com/gloss_frames

+ - / % <u>School</u> + = $ >

School is what – an institution for education? An arena for academic excellence? A home for learning the basic skills for success in life? Yeah…right! More like a fashion show, a wrestling ring, and the set for the Jerry Springer Show. School, besides being a place where you get educated, is a place for social interaction. Here is where you learn how to cooperatively work with other people, much like how you will be required to do for the rest of your life. You will forge friendships and relationships that could last your entire lifetime, while you benefit from getting to know people and from people getting to know you.

But if my assumptions are correct, schools nowadays have not changed much over time in regards to how we all socialize. I bet even in your school, there exist cliques, factions, and groups of friends that all hang out together. In some schools they are definite and impermeable - like when the "jocks" never talk to the "geeks", or the cheerleaders never talk to the "losers". In other schools, the social divisions are less apparent. The people there go outside of their primary friendship groups, but often regroup in settings like the cafeteria, the auditorium, and whenever a fight breaks out.

Wherever you are though, it is likely that people will naturally separate themselves based on interests, taste in clothing, ethnicity, and (yep, here it come) sexuality. Schools are known to give students who fit social stereotypes of a group a distinguished label. There's the "class clown", "the nerd", the "slut", and of course "the Gay guy". Trying to maintain a positive reputation at school can be a daunting task alone without the pressure of people knowing that you are Gay.

Oftentimes, students at predominately Black schools don't admit to their sexuality because they want to avoid having a stigma placed on them. For the Black student at the predominately non-Black school, he may already have the stigma of being a minority hanging over his head. And at mostly-Black schools, the climate of homophobia may seem at times to be written into the school's constitution. Black Gay students all over are closeted out of concern - fearing that if people knew that they were Gay, they may come to be known only by their sexuality. If someone is fairly popular and dreads being banished from their circle of friends just for being Gay, it is only natural that they conceal their full identity. Who wants to be made into an outcast? Not me, and I bet that you wouldn't want to be one either.

But I would also bet that the exact same reasoning of one student is shared by many others who are in the same predicament. No one is ever alone in fear. Although you may be afraid that you will lose all of your friends once they find out you're Gay, there is the possibility that one of your friends may fear that you will not like them because *they* are Gay. Coming out is said to be the most political of actions that a Gay person can take, because it says to the world "This is me; take it or leave it!" Others struggling with their sexuality may find strength in your courage, and decide that they too can be free from the dark and lonely closet.

There is strength in numbers. You would not be an outcast alone if you sought support from peers who are willing to fight against the same oppression. Coming out provides an incredible surge of relief and freedom. I understand that you may be at a time and/or place in your life where it would be better if you waited to come out, but do not use this as an excuse for not coming out forever. Growing up is a complicated process, especially when you're continually made to believe that your feelings are wrong. There are people and institutions that may damn you eternally just for being who you are, but the most promising thought is that ignorant people can change. If you take a stand and educated people – through forming Gay/Straight Alliances or engaging people in dialogues – the evils of bigotry and prejudice can end in time for us to witness it.

Building a Safe School

As a student, you have the right to learn in an environment that protects your safety. How many times in school have you heard someone equivocate something bad to being Gay: "Oh, this classroom is Gay; this pencil is Gay; this school is Gay!" You are probably subjected to verbal abuse all day, everyday, and you don't even realize it. Schools have the obligation to protect you from this. Black Gay students across the nation report that in their schools, there is an overwhelming anti-Gay atmosphere that is not only fostered by the students, but is rarely (if ever) addressed by the staff and faculty. What's worse is that there have been a number of students saying that the staff hosted homophobic comments and behaviors themselves. In your own school, you should not be abused by homophobic comments and blatant ignorance. You should not suffer being harassed by peers or authorities for being yourself. You should not be the object of ridicule or torment merely because everyone else doesn't understand you.

Access to money and power in this nation is obtained through getting an education. In order to survive, the Black man needs an education, yet the Black Gay man is often excluded from the opportunity of learning because of prejudice by both the powerful elite and his own people. So it's simple to say that if you want a place in the classroom, you're going to have to take it. Remind them of their purpose to leave "no child left behind". Make sure that your school provides a safe education for everyone, and that that is inclusive of the young Black Gay man striving to become something magnificent.

Ways to Combat Homophobia at School

1) Start a Gay-Straight Alliance

If you know of any other Gay people and/or Gay-friendly people, why not turn them into a collective body that works to reduce the school-wide climate of homophobia? It's a great way to meet new people, offer support to people who feel lonely, and provide information to anyone who has questions. A Gay-Straight Alliance (GSA) can be a fun way to establish Gay presence on your campus, and a constructive want to combat prejudices within your school. If you network with other Gay people, they are more likely to have your back in a rough situation

You can start a GSA by building up a group of people that are interested. About 10 is all you need to officially start one at your school. Once you have interested members, go about establishing your group the same way your institution requires other groups to become established. You may have to fill out a few forms, or get administration to OK it. Check your Student Handbook, or ask a guidance counselor for information that is specific to your school.

To keep the GSA going, consider the different people who would be in the group. Choose a meeting place that meets the needs of closeted students too, and include Gay, Lesbian, Bisexual, and Transgender issues into group plans. Advertise your group to get more people involved, but be aware of people who may come to the meetings just to find out who is Gay, etc. Word of mouth is usually ideal for the GSA on a very homophobic campus. To protect the safety of everyone, set up ground rules. Emphasize confidentiality, not labeling others, and mutual respect. The maintenance of the group's safety relies on how comfortable the members are.

2) Write to speakers to come to your school to discuss Gay issues

Many speakers will come to your school to speak – some will do it for free. Write to someone you think will help your cause and ask them to come talk to students about issues that concern you. The people you invite can range from active members of your school's surrounding community, professionals who are willing to tell a moralistic story, or a government official who will detail the importance of diversity and acceptance.

3) Raise awareness of Gays during Black History month

During Black History, urge people to include historical figures of prominence that were both Black and Gay in the celebration of our history. Bayard Rustin, Langston Hughes, and James Baldwin are a few to name, but you can also encourage them to explore and find more.

4) Try to get your school to celebrate GLBTQ History Month.

October is the month in which the history of Gays, Lesbians, Bisexuals, and Transgenders is honored. Ask the administrators, staff, and faculty if they will celebrate this, and if so, to include Black GLBTQ people of color.

5) Participate in the Day of Silence

Annually, students take a vow of silence for one day to pay tribute to the silence that the GLBTQ community has suffered for so long. Tell friends and teachers ahead of time of your plans, and encourage others to join you.

6) Ask administrators for staff development on teaching Gay students.

Let administrators know that the Gay students at your school are educationally underprivileged. This can be corrected by instructing teachers on how to tailor their classrooms to accommodate Gay students. See if GLBTQ issues can also be introduced into the curriculum.

7) Write your opinions in the school newspaper

School newspapers are always looking for information to distribute to the student body. This can be a way of getting your message across to wide audiences all at once (that is if anyone actually still reads the school newspaper)

8) Get staff & faculty to make "Safe Zone"s

Ask teachers to signify that their classroom is a safe zone for Gay students by hanging Gay supportive insignia in their rooms.

9) Ensure that all events are equal

Make sure that any functions, dances, and the proms are open to be attended by same-sex couples. If the school is having a dating auction, a same sex candidate should be eligible as well. Gay couples should be allowed to enjoy the benefits of prom and graduation equally to their heterosexual counterparts.

10) Push for GLBTQ related books in the library.

Seeing curriculum in which you can relate to is important in learning. Check to see if your library will include books with _positive_ Gay characters. Here are a few recommendations:

Books With _Your_ People in Them

"Gay Rebel of the Harlem Renaissance: Selections from the Work of Richard Bruce Nugent" by Bruce Nugent, Thomas H. Wirth, Richard Bruce Nugent

"The Greatest Taboo: Homosexuality in Black Communities" by Delroy Constantine-Simms

"Dangerous Liaisons: Blacks, Gays, and the Struggle for Equality" by Eric Brandt

"Respecting the Soul: Daily Reflections for Black Lesbians and Gays" by Keith Boykin

"I'm on My Way" by Christopher David

"Black Like Us: A Century of Lesbian, Gay, and Bisexual African American Fiction" by Devon W. Carbado

"Go the Way Your Blood Beats: An Anthology of Lesbian and Gay Fiction by African-American Writers" by Shawn Stewart Ruff

"Fighting Words: Personal Essays by Black Gay Men" by Charles Michael Smith

"Black, Gay & Christian: (An Inspirational Guidebook to Daily Living)" by Herndon L. Davis

"In the Life: A Black Gay Anthology" by Joseph Beam

"Fresh Men: New Voices in Gay Fiction" by Edmund White, Don Weise

"Words of Fire: Essays by Black Gay Writers" by Charles Michael Smith

Teachers that wish to make students aware that their classroom is a "Safe Zone" for GLBTQ student may hang up this poster to let all students know that homophobia is not allowed:

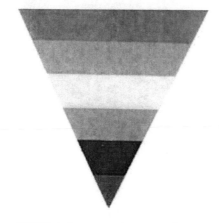

ALLY

SAFE ZONE

Supporting the Dignity
of All People

For the College Man

Being a Black Gay man in college is a lot easier than being a Black Gay man in high school. With entry into college you are granted freedoms and responsibilities far greater than what you may have possessed as a teenager under your parents' rule. But, that is not to say that in college you will not face difficulties because you are Gay and Black. The problems circling your race and sexuality do not lessen, they just change. In college, some still decide not to be out to their parents. Or people who were out at their high schools may decide not to be as overt in college. College presents the young Black Gay man with a horde of opportunities, while simultaneously giving him an assortment of decisions he will have to make.

One issue facing college-enrolled Black Gay men is the decision to be openly Gay. College is a place where people network to make life-long friends and future business partners. The business world is notorious for its perpetuation of institutional racism. Blacks on the corporate ladder are significantly outnumbered by their white male counterpart, and are disadvantaged because of racist notions that cause employers to see Blacks as incompetent and subordinate. For a student to divulge that, in addition to being Black, that he is Gay seems, to many, to be undertaking an extra burden. To be Black is one disadvantage in the corporate climate; to be Gay is another. The combination of these two identities causes the Black Gay male to feel that he must choose the characteristic he most obviously identifies with (Black), while suppressing his other identity (Gay).

On campus, Black Gay men also fear exploitation because of their sexuality. Black Gay men have habitually been anxious amidst fraternity life because of the popular climate of strict heterosexuality that fraternities encourage. Fraternities promote heterosexist dominance with parties that objectify women, explicit jokes about heterosexual prowess and behavior, and activities seen as masculine and male-oriented. Black Gay men who want to join fraternities for merit, social benefits, or to fully enjoy the college experience face the option of being closeted and accepted, or out and rejected.

Fear of physical abuse also lingers in the psyche of the Black Gay college student. In 2002, at Morehouse College a Black Gay man was beaten severely with a baseball bat when a floor-mate claimed that the Gay man was staring at him while he showered. Before and during the beating, the attacker was noted saying "Faggot, you're Gay, Gay. . . . I hate these Morehouse faggots." Homophobic sentiment on campus can often lead to homophobic actions, and this fact has Black Gay men in college concealing their sexuality in fear.

Financial dependence also causes Black Gay men to face internal turmoil while in college. Most college students receive assistance in paying the college bill from their parents. In some situations, Gay Black men worry that if it were to become known to their parents that they were Gay, the parents would stop investing money into their Gay son's college education. In other situations, the parents know about their child's sexuality, but as a clause for paying the term bill, the son must agree to keep his sexual orientation a secret.

Covert acts of anti-Gay prejudice also terrorize black Gay men in college. As a Black Gay student, homophobia has the potential to be a factor when your teacher grades your paper, when you run for office in a campus organization, or in whether an internship employer decides to hire you. Fear that a homophobic teacher may be assert anti-Gay bias while grading their papers makes Black Gay college men even more compelled to conceal their identity.

The Black Gay man living on a college campus has even more to worry about if he has a roommate. Will his roommate be comfortable with his sexuality if he knows about it? Will his roommate become problematical if the Gay Black man decides to bring his same-sex partner to the room? Are there certain boundaries that should be set about nudity and privacy? All of these are questions that plague Black Gay men at colleges and universities across the nation, and they require careful consideration to be resolved efficiently.

A college education is almost as much a necessity as air and water are, if one wants to be successful in life. Enrollment at an institution for higher learning should provide a safe learning environment for all students – especially with the high costs we pay for them. College is an investment, and like any investment you make, you have to protect it. Knowing what you can do to survive in the college setting will help you, as a Black Gay man, to protect that which is so sacred – your education.

Financial Resources for Black Gay Students

The first part of going to college is paying for it. Whether your parents are going to assist you in paying for college, or you are in a situation where your parents will not support you financially, it never hurts to know how you can get free money to pay for college. There are tons of scholarships waiting to give the educated Black Gay man financial opportunity. Here are a few ways you can get it.

WEBSITES	SCHOLARSHIPS
lgbtcampus.org	• Audre Lorde Scholarship Fund (Georgia)
finaid.org	• African American Community Coalition Scholarship Awards
finaid.org/otheraid/Gay.phtml	• American Library Association Scholarship for Minorities
fastweb.com	• CSWS Laurel Research Award
www.ngltf.org/about/messenger.htm	• Colgate/Palmolive Dental Scholarship
www.league-att.org/foundation	• Ebony Scholarship
www.colinhiggins.org	• Minorities' Job Bank
www.colage.org/scholarship.html	• National Achievement Scholarship Program for Outstanding Negros
www.tself.org	• Equity Foundation
www.react.com/take_action/faq.html	• Gay and Lesbian Medical Association
www.ngltf.org/about/messenger.htm	• The LEAGUE Foundation Academic Scholarships
www.ngpa.org/education.html	• OUT Magazine Matthew Shepard Scholarship Fund
www.college-scholarships.com	• National Gay Lesbian Task Force (NGLTF) Fellowships
www.guaranteed-scholarships.com	Pride Foundation (Pacific Northwest)
www.scholarship.org	
www.carpedm.com	
MAILING ADDRESS	
Fund for Lesbian and Gay Scholarships	
213-650-5752	
PO Box 48320	
Los Angeles, CA 90048-0320	

Tips to Succeed on Campus

Being a Black Gay man in college is an honorable accomplishment. You have made a huge step in life's journey and you should be really proud of yourself. But, getting into college is only the beginning of the battle. The ultimate goal is to eventually walk out of there with a degree. The Black Gay college man should adhere to certain guidelines in order to graduate from college and elevate himself to even higher levels. Here are a few survival tips for the Black Gay man in college:

Stay organized. There is a stereotype about how Gay men are all naturally neat and organized; but sadly, this fails to ring true for *all* of us. However, practice makes perfect. Begin organizing yourself, and you will find that the tasks you have to complete will become easier. Invest in a planner in which you can write down important dates, exam days, due dates, and other events.

Prioritize. Friends can convince you to go anywhere, especially when you're in the middle of studying something that is boring. Be firm with your obligations and stay focused. Keep what's important at the top of your "to do" list.

Get accustomed to the campus setting. Know where your classes are, what time the library opens, and the quickest route from point A to point B. The Black Gay college man should be campus-savvy like no one else.

One of the most important things you can do in college is "be there". Attendance is not mandatory all of the time, but that doesn't mean it's not necessary. Whether you have class, a sport, a meeting, or an event - be there, and be there on time (maybe even a little earlier to get prepared).

Preparation is vital in college. Go to class having already read the book. Turn assignments in on or ahead of deadlines. Follow the class syllabus and understand what *is* going on in class and what *will* be going on in class.

Study. In high school many students succeed without ever studying. In college, without studying, you are likely to flunk out the first semester. You must know the information enough to explain it yourself, not just memorize it. Tutors are accessible if help is need.

Don't separate school and the rest of your life. Take what you learned and look for examples in real life. Talk about what you learned with someone else. Immerse yourself in what you are learning and you, yourself, will become learned.

Set a high standard for yourself. Aim for the dean's list or to be best in the class. This motivates you to work to be the best. Avoid laziness and procrastination – both are downfalls to the academic student.

Mingle. Use the knowledge and experiences of others to increase your own. Join study groups of intent people, and get to know interesting people. Joining a club is an excellent way to see people, be seen, and form lasting bonds.

Get to know your professor and let them get to know you. It may sway their grading in your favor if they empathize with you. Also, their title may come in handy when you need a letter of recommendation for a job, internship, or scholarship.

Be cordial to people. Represent yourself positively. College is a place where you never know who you might need someday. Do not "burn bridges" with people who may be able to lend you a hand in the future.

Don't be too stubborn to ask for help. College is designed to be a challenge, and with that in mind, the college recognizes that a mental struggle will help the student grow. Colleges and universities offer tutors, assistants, academic counselors, advisors, and many people all willing to help you succeed in your academic endeavors. They're paid for by your tuition, so you might as well utilize them.

Take care of yourself. Your parents and guardians are not there to monitor your eating or health, so you are now your guardian. Maintain a healthy diet, and visit the hospital or campus health center when necessary. Being busy is no excuse for you to let your body deteriorate.

With the challenges of college, stress comes naturally. Practice stress reduction. Find something you enjoy doing and do it to relax yourself periodically. Have fun. College at times may seem overwhelming, but you have to remind yourself that you are not a robot – you're a human. Enjoying yourself and making time for pleasure aids the Black Gay college student in understanding the balance between freedom and responsibility.

Top Colleges

There are hundreds of colleges and universities that have been named to have the best environment for a specific type of student. Columbia University, New York University and Brown University make up a few of the top colleges with the most accepting atmosphere for Gays; while Morehouse, Howard University, and Florida A&M University have been named the best institutions for Black men. But what is the ideal school for the Black Gay man? Surely, on the campuses deemed "best place for GLBTQ community members" have a degree of racism on campus. Just as historically Black colleges often possess a climate of intolerance towards Gays. So what is the Black Gay man searching for a comfortable place of learning to do?

Finding a college that fits you is extremely important. Many factors, such as size, location, and curriculum, all play a role in your decision to attend the university of your choice. Lists ranking colleges for Blacks and Gays are based solely off of research measuring a college's overall setting. The "best school for Blacks" or the "best school for Gays" may not be the best school for you. College is what you make of it. So whatever college you choose, make sure that it fits you comfortably and allows for you to expand your knowledge in a safe and productive milieu. A college that is not on either list might be a great choice for you, serving both as a place for you to get a great education and make a difference by enhancing the schools' diversity.

In the Church

One of the most difficult aspects of a Black Gay man's life can be the struggles that he faces spiritually. Churches - and religions in general - have a long-running history of anti-Gay preaching which has consistently told parishioners that homosexuality is a sin. Religious grounds are at the forefront of most homophobically based arguments, but the scripture is being incorrectly interpreted and used to wreak havoc on the spirits of Black Gay men who practice faith.

Religion is supposed to serve as a body of support; meant to give us hope when we feel hopeless. The belief that God will accept you when no one else will has been undermined by ignorant worshipers who continually use the Bible as a weapon for discrimination, judgment, and bigotry. And if the damage done by other people wasn't bad enough, the Black Gay worshipper must face his own internal mayhem of the seemingly clashing aspects of his identity. Black Gay religious youth sometimes fear that every time they feel attraction to another boy, they are condemned by God. Or that every time they engage in sexual activity with their same-sex partner, they are sentenced to spend eternity in damnation. Black Gay youth who are avid followers of "the gospel" often feel forced to choose between their passion in the church, and their emotional happiness.

This, I say, is the *real* abomination. The overall message of religion is of love for everyone. As a Black Gay Christian, you may have to remind people of this from time to time. Religion can be a beautiful thing when used to better the goodness of mankind. To survive in the face of those attempting to misguided religious conviction to build walls, here are a few tools that you can use to knock those walls down.

The Truth: Sexual Orientation Is NOT Mentioned In The Bible

Modern-day definitions on sexual orientation did not exist during biblical times. In fact, sexuality in general is seldom discussed in the Bible. What the Bible does discuss are relationships in terms of women's role as men's possessions, the obligation of procreation, the expectations of a married male and female, and the sustenance of a male-dominated society, all specifically conferred in Genesis 38.

The mind of the anti-Gay worshipper is so narrow that most of them rely on the same sources to preach intolerance, There are six scriptures habitually used to dehumanize the Gay community: Genesis 19:5, Leviticus 18:22, Leviticus 20:13, Romans 1:26-27, I Corinthians 6:9, and I Timothy 1:9-10. As part of your survival, I present you with the scriptures used, and the truth behind each message.

To effectively combat claims that these verses support homosexual inferiority, I would encourage you to read the entire chapter and familiarize yourself with it. For Romans 1:26-27, read the first 3 chapters of Romans. You may also want to read Genesis chapter 38 for a clear picture of the Old Testament attitudes about women, sex, the necessity of producing offspring, the control of men over women, the double standard for men and women, and other lifestyle issues.

Genesis 19:5:

"Bring them out to us that we may know them."

Modern versions of the Bible have reworded the phrase "know" to mean "has sex with". The original text reads "know", and it should be interpreted to mean "know"- to have information. No hint at homosexuality exists in the original Hebrew scripture, and no later Bible refers to homosexuality as the sin of Sodom. The word "know" in Genesis 19:5 is Hebrew YADA. It is used 943 times in the Old Testament to "know" God, good and evil, the truth, the law, people, places, things, etc. It is a very flexible word, as are many Hebrew words. In Genesis 19:5, the word was used to express the request of the people of Sodom that Lot should bring out the strangers in his house so that they could know who they were. Sodom was a tiny fortress in the barren wasteland south of the Dead Sea. The only strangers that the people of Sodom ever saw were enemy tribes who wanted to destroy and take over their valuable fortress and the trade routes that it protected. Lot himself was an alien in their midst.

The word "Sodom" comes from the story of Sodom, but the word itself is not a biblical word. Laws against sodomy use an incorrect and wrongly translated term for the laws. A "Sodomite" in the Bible is simply a person who lives in Sodom, which included Lot and his family. The term "sodomite" in the King James Version of Deuteronomy 23:17 and I Kings 14:24 is an incorrect translation of the Hebrew word for "temple prostitute."

The unknowing Bible reader assumes that the Bible clearly condemns homosexual intercourse as "sodomy" and that the city of Sodom was destroyed because of homosexuality. These assumptions are, however, based on no evidence found in the Bible. None of the biblical references to Sodom mention sexual sins but, but instead condemn Sodom for its injustice, lack of hospitality to strangers, idolatry and as a symbol for desolation and destruction.

As a way to appease the men of Sodom at Lot's door, Lot offered his young daughters to the men. If the men were homosexual, why would he offer his daughters? The sin of the men at Lot's door was their hostility and violence. Their sexual orientation was irrelevant.

To twist the story to say what it does not say is to miss what it does say. The story does not deal with sexual orientation or with homosexuality and has no bearing at all on the issue of God's acceptance or rejection of Gays and Lesbians. The purpose of the story is to show that misunderstood, strange, or feared minorities in any community are in danger from violence by the majority when that majority is ignorant, ungodly, selfish and afraid. The story of Sodom clearly teaches that evil and violent people who attack stranger whom they fail to understand receive God's punishment.

Leviticus 18:22:

"You shall not lie with a male as those who lie with a female; it is an abomination."

Leviticus 20:13:

"If a man lies with a male as those who lie with a woman, both of them have committed an abomination and they shall surely be put to death."

These two versus, possibly the most commonly used to debase homosexuality, misconstrues the two individuals involved in the sexual act. Both of these verses refer, not to homosexuals, but to heterosexuals who took part in the banal fertility rituals in order to guarantee good crops and healthy flocks. The word abomination in Leviticus refers to (1) things considered to be religiously unclean or (2) things associated with idol worship. Thus, these scriptures state that having Gay sex only to appease to a crop-assuring deity is wrong – not that Gay sex itself is wrong.

Additionally, the praying to of a god for crops is not relevant in modern times. The Bible condemns many acts that are currently acceptable. The use of Leviticus to condemn and reject homosexuals is irrelevant in a time that has changed significantly since the times in which the Bible was written.

Look at Leviticus 11:1-12, where all "unclean" animals are forbidden as food - including rabbits, pigs, and shellfish, such as oysters, shrimp, lobsters, crabs, and clams. Anyone who argues for the validity of Leviticus should attack seafood distributors as equally as they attack homosexuals.

Leviticus 12:1-8 states that a woman is "unclean" for 33 days after giving birth to a boy and for 66 days after giving birth to a girl and goes on to demand that certain animals must be sacrificed as an offering for "religious cleansing". Today's religious advocates do not advocate for this practice as equally as they do for the oppression of Gays.

Leviticus 23 details regulations concerning "complete rest" on the Sabbath day and demands of animal sacrifices to be carried out according to exact instructions. Leviticus 18:19 forbids a husband from having sex with his wife during her menstrual period. Leviticus 19:19 forbids mixed breeding of various kinds of cattle, the sowing of various kinds of seeds in a field, or the wearing of "a garment made from two kinds of material mixed together." Leviticus 19:27 demands that "you shall not round off the side-growth of your heads, nor harm the edges of your beard." The next verse forbids "tattoo marks on yourself." The Bible sets forth a number of rules and regulations for its followers, but hardly ever are they all strictly followed.

The Bible also condemns those who do not enforce its laws equally, as well as those who pass judgment on other when they themselves have flaws. Jesus never condemned homosexuals. Jesus, in Matthew 7:1-5 said, "Do not judge lest you be judged yourselves...", and yet the bulk of religious Gay-bashers uphold their essence of hypocrisy. So you can see that it is those who misuse the Bible to teach rejection who are the true sinners.

Romans 1:26-27:

"For this reason God gave them over to degrading passions: for their women exchanged the natural use for that which is against nature. And in the same way also the men abandoned the natural use of the woman and burned in their desire toward one another, men with men committing indecent acts and receiving in their own persons the due penalty for their error."

The crime that this text refers to is idolatry of anyone but God. This scripture was written by Paul, in a time when idolatrous religious practices were common. The text is part of Paul's criticism of idol worship, which may have been specifically known to Paul's readers during his era. However, today the argument is vague and indirect to us. Paul's writings have been taken out of context and twisted to punish and oppress every identifiable minority in the world: Jews, children, women, Blacks, slaves, politicians, divorced people, convicts, Lesbians, Gays, religious reformers, the mentally ill, etc. Paul's writing is very difficult to translate because, since most of his letters were written in response to news from other people, reading Paul can be like listening to one side of a telephone conversation. Reasonable translations of Paul's text exist, but we are unconscious to what is being said on the other side.

Romans 1:26-27 contains some words that only Paul uses, in addition to words that are common, but given a different meaning by Paul. The word "passions" in 1:26 is the same word used to speak of the suffering and death of Jesus in Acts 1:3 and does not mean what we mean by "passion" today. Eros is the Greek word for romantic love, and could have been used to describe "passion", but it wasn't. "Passions" in 1:26 likely refers to the frenzied state of mind that many ancient mystery cults induced in worshipers by means of wine, drugs, and music.

The term "against nature" is also misinterpreted to mean unnatural. Since the same term is used by Paul in Romans 11:21-24 to speak of God acting "against nature" by including the Gentiles with the Jews in the family of God, we assert that Paul's meaning for "against nature" refers to something not done in the usual way. Something done against one's nature is something done that they do not usually do. Example: After growing my hair for two years, going to the barber was against my nature. The implication that any acts were unnatural is unfounded and untrue.

"Committing indecent acts" in 1:27 is translated by King James Version as "working that which is unseemly." This word for "indecency" was used to translate Deuteronomy 24:1 into Greek to say that a man could divorce his wife if he "found some indecency in her." The religious teachers argued endlessly about what "some indecency" meant. Some said it was anything that displeased the husband. Others were more strict and said it could only refer to adultery. The crime being committed in Paul's text is adultery, not homosexuality.

Paul was certainly aware of the variety of ways that the word "indecency" could be interpreted, and he used it in a variety of ways himself. To label "indecent acts" purely as a homosexual reference is nothing more than reckless speculation. If Paul had intended to condemn homosexuals, he certainly possessed the literary skill to do so clearly. As in the rest of the Bible, Paul nowhere even hints that Gay people can or should change their sexual orientation. What is said by Paul is that "the gospel is the power of God for spiritual freedom (salvation) for all who believe." (Romans 1:16).

I Corinthians 6:9:

"The unrighteous shall not inherit the kingdom of God. So do not be deceived; neither fornicators, nor idolaters, nor adulterers, nor effeminate, nor homosexuals, nor thieves, nor covetous, nor drunkards, nor revilers, nor swindlers, shall inherit the realm of God."

I Timothy 1:9-10:

"Law is not made for a righteous person but for those who are lawless and rebellious, for the ungodly and sinners, for the unholy and profane, for those who kill their fathers or mothers, for murderers and fornicators and homosexuals and kidnappers and liars and perjurers, and whatever else is contrary to sound (healthy) teaching."

The bigotry and condemnation of Gays based of this scripture comes from the inaccurate translation of two words: "homosexual" and "effeminate".
Again, I remind you that neither of these words existed at or near the time in which the Bible was written, so modern-day meanings of the word are included in place of the REAL words used. There is no word in biblical Greek or Hebrew that is parallel to the word "homosexual." No Bible before the Revised Standard Version in 1946 used "homosexual" in any Bible translation.

The word translated as "homosexual" is Greek "arsenokoites", which was formed from two words meaning "male" and "bed". This word is not found anywhere else in the Bible and has not been found anywhere in the contemporary Greek of Paul's time. It likely denotes a male prostitute with female customers, which was a common practice in the Roman world, as revealed in the excavations at Pompeii and other sites.

The word translated "effeminate in 1 Corinthians 6:9 is Greek "malakoi", which means "soft" or "vulnerable." The word is translated as "soft" in reference to clothing in Matthew 11:8 and Luke 7:25 and as "illness" in Matthew 4:23 and 9:35. It is not used anywhere else in the New Testament and carries no hint of reference to sexual orientation. "Malakoi" in 1 Corinthians 6:9 probably refers to those who are "soft," "pliable," "unreliable," or "without courage or stability." The translation of malakoi as "effeminate" is incorrect, ignorant, degrading to women, and impossible to justify based on ancient usage compared to the meaning of "effeminate" today.

This incorrect rendering of "malakoi" and "arsenokoites" as references to sexual orientation has been ruinous to the lives of Black Gay men in churches everywhere. Inaccurate translations of ancient texts have served to marginalize our community long enough. To end the fear and hatred incited by ignorance, you have to be willing and prepared to confront and correct it. Key to the *spiritual* survival of the Black Gay youth is knowing that half the battle is won when you, yourself, become enlightened.

You vs. The Church

For those looking to bring change to your entire church, here are six steps you can take to combat homophobia in your "House of God":

1. Become acquainted with your congregation, and the leaders at your church. Knowing the political hierarchy of your institution is good in trying to establish communication.

2. A group of people speaks louder than one. Try to locate other members of your church who may have similar issues. If you can't find other Black Gay parishioners, invite some into the church to join you in your cause. Administrators sometimes overlook individuals, but they can't ignore the needs of many.

3. Peace should be kept in dealing with the head of your ministry. Avoid heated debates over homosexuality, but instead focus on your concerns for equality. People are more likely to give you what you want when you approach them coolly, intelligibly, and respectfully.

4. If no others are willing to help your struggle, have the courage to overcome problems single-handedly. Be fully prepared to be outed and even preached against by name. Hardships are expected when change is made. Have confidence in knowing that the change you make affects not only you, but all those who feel marginalized by the church – whether they openly admit it or not.

5. The battle for equality transcends just Black Gay people in your church. Find straight supporters who can usher in justice along with you. Heterosexual urgency for equality is crucial in letting everyone know that no one should be left out in church.

6. Avoid arguments over specific scriptures when talking with members of the clergy. Do not debate Scripture or the interpretation of Scripture. Provide them with literature that supports your beliefs, but also remind them that acceptance of everyone is God's word. Include accounts of your own personal experiences, and how you maintain a relationship with God just like all the other worshippers of your church.

PROTECT YOURSELF

Hate is a viscous thing. Prejudice alone is the thought of treating someone harshly because of their difference. Discrimination is when this thought turns into action. Racially and/or sexually motivated crimes are common in the world. As a Black Gay man, there will be people who look to do you harm, whether it be emotionally, verbally, psychologically, or physically. In any even, you should know how to protect yourself as a component of your survival. There are many means for you to ensure yourself of safety, and to make it past the harm that people want to commit against you. Be strong, be smart, and be ready at a moment's notice. Your life as a Black Gay man may depend on it.

Walking Safely

Whenever you are walking to go somewhere, be aware of loiterers. Try not to travel anywhere alone, especially if it is dark. At night, travel only streets that are well-lit and have other people walking on them. Do not hitchhike, or accept rides from strangers. Unless absolutely necessary, avoid walking with large amounts of cash or flashy, expensive jewelry.

Walk on the side of the street in the direction of oncoming traffic, and walk on sidewalks – not the street. Be weary of people in cars asking for directions. Maintain a polite, but safe distance when talking to strangers in a car. If confronted by someone in a car, run in the direction opposite the way the car is facing.

When you get to your destination, particularly if it is dark, don't hang around the entrance. If at home, quickly check for mail or newspapers, and go inside. If you feel suspicious of the place, don't let the door close behind you. Get away and seek assistance. If you feel someone is following you or watching you intently, go to the nearest occupied residence or building, and ask for help. If someone does confront you, yell "FIRE!" instead of "Help!" (People are more willing to run to a fire to help than to run to someone actually screaming for help). If you need accessories to help you feel safe, you should carry a police whistle, a flashlight, or pepper spray/mace where they're readily available. Always make sure it's not prohibited where you are going (Do not go to school with a can of mace unless you want a free trip to jail).

Safety on Mass Transit

When you're waiting for a bus, train, or cab, stand near the other people waiting with you. If no one is waiting with you, and the area is dark, stand near an occupied building or under a street light. Once your transportation has arrived, be aware of who is driving and who is riding with you. If someone looks or acts suspicious, notify the driver, or other transit personnel, or call the police.

If you get on an empty or near-empty bus or train, sitting close to the driver can make you feel safer. If a fellow-rider harasses you, let the driver or ticket-handlers know immediately. When you get off at your stop, be aware of those who stop with you. If you feel you are being followed, go to the nearest occupied building and ask for help. At night, try to get off in areas that are well-lit, and walk on streets that are illuminated.

911

You can always call 911 for free from a payphone or cell phone. If a situation calls for emergency assistance, dial 9-1-1 immediately. If you are calling from a house, the 911 operator may automatically know the address you are calling from, the telephone number, and the name of the person whose telephone line it is, so the police can be sent to your location even if you don't get a chance to request it.

Robbery

Naturally, nobody wants to give up what belongs to them. But it's important to remember that you should never resist if you are the victim of a robbery. Do exactly what they want you to do. They don't want to be there any longer than you want them to, so quickly comply and your chances of remaining unharmed will be greater. Important though, is for you to get a good look at the assailant so that you can describe them to the police, and action can be taken.

Whatever the robber takes can be replaced. Your life cannot. Staying alive is your #1 priority. Mentally record the robber's height, weight, facial features, attire, and which way he escaped. This information could potentially lead to an arrest that gets you your possessions back and stops this crime from happening to someone else.

What to do if you are harassed

If you become the target of anti-Gay harassment (or witness it on someone else) here are some appropriate ways in which you can respond:

Know that you are not to blame. Victimization is never a justifiable reason for anything.

Find someone you trust to talk to about it. Venting will help you feel better and prepare for action to address the harassment.

Assert yourself and make your boundaries known. Let it be understood that the harassment is inappropriate and will not be tolerated.

Understand what rights you have. Know how you can use authorities to remedy the problem. Avoid vigilantism – that is, trying to solve the problem through illegal methods such as fighting, threatening, or revenge.

File a complaint with the proper authorities, whether it be staff, managers, parents, or police. Know exactly what happened, what was wrong, and what you want to be done about it.

Document the event. A record of the incident will be useful in remembering the details of the situation, and presenting it to authorities. Even with little incident, you should record them, because they may someday be useful in proving that smaller action lead to more threatening ones. Do not be afraid to ask for help.

National Anti-Violence Prevention Hotline: 1-800-616-HATE

Fighting Back

Generally speaking, Black Gay men are lovers, not fighters. I too prefer resolving problems through thoughts and dialogue. But the people out there who have it ingrained in their heads that they want to do harm to Black and/or Gay men are beyond logic. So as much as I detest violence of any sort, I detest even worse victimization. Thus, in the event that you are backed against the proverbial wall, I feel you should be knowledgeable of certain moves you can use to protect yourself and get to safety. When you need to turn to violence in order to combat it, here are 4 tips that will thwart the victimization of another member of the Black Gay community:

TIP #1 - USE YOUR HEAD

Your brain is the most powerful weapon you have, in any situation. Tell yourself to remain calm and think. After adrenaline begins, your body will tense up, and your brain will try to react with the first thought that pops into your head. If you are grabbed, bear-hug style from behind, don't attempt to step on the attacker's toes, elbow his ribs, or kick your heel into his groin. These moves are ineffective and will only make your attacker angrier. Your head is also a powerful weapon in that it can be used by bashing the back of your head into the attacker's nose. If you connect once or twice with a hard bash, the attacker will be effectively hurt.

TIP #2 - ALWAYS HAVE A TOOL HANDY

Absolutely do not walk around with illegal weapons! But that's not to say that you have to be unarmed. Everyday tools can be used in your defense if a dangerous situation arises. Pens, keys, rings, and other objects can be crafty and quickly accessible tools that aid in protecting yourself.

If you remember this one simple rule about weapons fighting, you will see the potential weapon in virtually everything around you and be able to effectively use it: anything hard and fast goes to bone, and anything pointed goes to soft tissue.

For example, a stick or can of vegetables would target bone: the face, skull, hip, shin, elbow, or kneecap. It would be less effective to use these against, say, an attacker's abdomen. Conversely, a knife or pen is much more effective targeting the throat, eyes, crotch, armpit, or belly than they are targeting the kneecap.

"Hard to bone, sharp to flesh" - remember that rule, and you will never be without a weapon again.

TIP #3 - MOVE ALONG A TRIANGLE

When fighting there's one thing you don't want to do: get hit. One way of avoiding an attacker's advances is the "triangle theory" - the theory of moving your in a triangular pattern to avoid an attacker's punches.

One of the most dangerous mistakes the average person makes during a fight is moving in straight lines - either forward and backward, or side to side. Imagine a vertical dividing line along your body, dividing your body into left and right halves. The attacker is most likely to attack some point along or around that line near the center of your body - your face, your throat, your heart, or your groin.

To effectively thwart an attacker's hits, you have to constantly shift that line out of the path of the attack *and* change the distance of the target from attacker. The attacker has mentally committed to striking a particular target. His brain has sent the signal to his fist that the intended target is located at a particular distance in a particular direction. When you change the target's coordinates, it spoils the effectiveness of the attack.

Imagine standing with both feet on the point of a triangle, facing the attacker. The other two points of the triangle can either be in front of you or behind you. Now imagine the other triangle points at about one medium-large step away from your starting point.

Step one foot onto either of the two available triangle points. Moving in a straight line backward and forward changes the distance, but does not move your center line out of the attack path. Moving laterally changes the location of the center line, but not the distance. Moving along an imaginary triangle changes both. The attacker may be able to recover from a change in target location or change in target distance alone, but changing both factors is your best bet. Then, even if it does connect, the strength of the attack will be greatly diminished.

TIP #4 - ALWAYS ADVANCE WHEN YOU SHOULD RETREAT
Like chess, fighting involves planning your moves ahead of time as well as the moves of your opponent. Most fighters' moves are a series of repeated moves that they have thought of ahead of time that will yield a desired reaction out of you. The attacker has in their mind already that after they attack you will retreat. DON'T. Fight your own instinct and do not back up. Your instinct is wrong.

The element of surprised is crucial in battle. How surprised will your attacker be when, after he attacks you, you quickly retaliate? While the attacker tries to figure out how to handle this unexpected happening, you keep the retaliation going until you have overcome the attacker. Then get to a safe place and seek help.

Source: http://womencentral.net/defense-tips.html

LAW

America is a wonderful country. The halls of democracy ring with the sound of justice for everyone. Wait, is that right? Hmm. Do laws grant life, liberty, and the pursuit of happiness to *every* man? Does US legislation indoctrinate the ideal of all men created equal being afforded inalienable rights to *all*? Well, I guess not. The United States, since its establishment in 1776, has sworn to uphold the equality of all of its citizens, yet throughout history we can continually see the hypocrisy enacted against different groups. Japanese immigrants were banished to internment camps, women were denied the right to vote, and let's not forget the "big one" – the kidnap and enslavement of Black Africans to build this country.

AS long as humans exist, injustices will continue to happen until we realize that other people's differences should not yield persecution. Currently, the Gay community is the bearer of most of the US's legal injustices. Gays who are willing to fight and die for their country are not allowed to be open about who they are in the military. Criminals who brutalize people because of their sexuality go unpunished for their hate crimes against the GLBTQ community. Discrimination in the workplace based on sexual orientation is permitted in most states. The problems faced by GLBTQ youth often go avoided and disregarded. Committed same-sex partners are denied the right to enter into legally binding marriages that will protect the welfare of their family. The list goes on.

Laws in this country are far from being inclusive to all of the members of the United States, and for this, I believe that it is necessary for the GLBTQ community, and more specifically, the Black Gay community, to be aware of what laws exist – federally and locally – that can either hinder your livelihood or defend your dignity.

Gay Youth and Schools

Public schools are pressured to prohibit any Gay-positive messages to young people, even while anti-Gay violence against students is widespread. Gay students' freedom of speech is often suppressed by homophobic administrators. Pro-Gay pupils, teachers, and their allies are often made the target of harassment and acts of violence or vandalism.

"Don't Ask, Don't Tell"

One of the nation's largest employers of young Black men is the military. Black Gay men are not allowed to admit that they are homosexual without being banned from the military, thanks to the "Don't Ask, Don't Tell." This means that no one can ask you if you are Gay, and you cannot tell, show, or act as if you are Gay. Gay men have made tremendous sacrifices in the US armed forces just like everyone else in the military. They deserve to be judged by the same standards as all others, which is a right guaranteed by the nation's constitution.

Antidiscrimination Laws

Only seventeen of the fifty states, plus Washington D.C. have laws that protect Gay employees from discrimination in the workplace. Only five states include clauses that protect transgenders and/or people who may face discrimination based on gender identity. Nationally, several local governments have also adopted civil rights ordinances inclusive of Gays and Lesbians in employment, public accommodations, housing, credit, union practices, and education.

Here is a map of the US in relation to the states' anti-discrimination legislation:

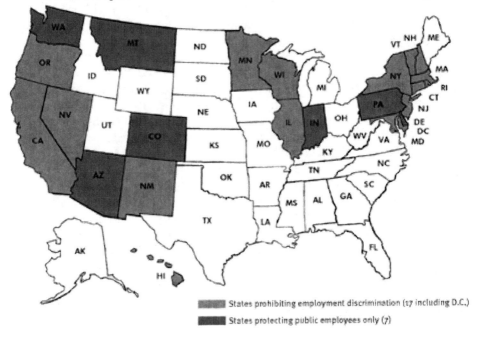

States prohibiting employment discrimination (17 including D.C.)
States protecting public employees only (7)

Source: http://www.lambdalegal.org/cgi-bin/iowa/states/antidiscrimi-map

Age of Consent Laws

The age of consent – the minimum age at which laws allows you to engage in sexual activity – is a touchy subject. People have an image of youth as "innocent", and visualizing them in the act of sex can be well, sickening. This emotion of disgust is what causes people to hold reservations about when you should be having sex, who you should be having sex with, and how old the person you are having sex with is. Sex is a physical and psychological activity. And, for example, there are evident differences between the physical and emotional maturity of a 16-year-old, versus the physical and emotional maturity of a 25-year-old. Consequently, the union of such people is seen by most, as a taboo.

But attraction is attraction. Regardless of whether you like older men, or prefer younger guys, you should be aware of the legal limitations imposed on your dating. It may feel right when you're with him, but simply engaging in the act of love-making could put you or him behind bars if you two are found out, and legal action is taken. Know the laws and try to stay out of situations that could lead to harm on either partner.

UNITED STATES AGE OF CONSENT LAWS

State	Male/Female Sex	Male/Male Sex
Alabama	16	Law invalidated
Alaska	16	16
Arizona	18	law repealed
Arkansas	16	Law invalidated
California	18	18
Colorado	15	17
Connecticut	15	16
D.C.	16	Law Repealed
Delaware	16	Law Repealed
Florida	16	Law invalidated
Georgia	16	16
Hawaii	14	Law Repealed
Idaho	16	Law invalidated
Illinois	17	17
Indiana	16	16
Iowa	18	Law Repealed
Kansas	16	Law invalidated
Kentucky	16	Law invalidated
Louisiana	17	Law invalidated
Maine	16	16
Maryland	16	Law invalidated
Massachusetts	16	Law invalidated
Michigan	16	Law invalidated
Minnesota	16	Law invalidated
Mississippi	16	Law invalidated
Missouri	17	Law invalidated
Montana	16	18
Nebraska	17	Law Repealed
Nevada	16	18
New Hampshire	16	18
New Jersey	16	16
New Mexico	17	17
New York	17	17
North Carolina	16	Law invalidated
North Dakota	18	Law repealed
Ohio	16	Law Repealed
Oklahoma	16	Law invalidated
Oregon	18	18
Pennsylvania	16	16
Rhode Island	16	Law repealed
South Carolina	14	Law invalidated
South Dakota	16	Law Repealed
Tennessee	18	Law Invalidated
Texas	17	Law invalidated
Utah	16	Law invalidated
Vermont	16	Law Repealed
Virginia	16	Law invalidated
Washington	16	16
West Virginia	16	18
Wisconsin	18	18
Wyoming	16	Law repealed

Source: http://www.avert.org/aofconsent.htm

Birth Certificate Amendments

People born with physical genitalia opposite of their gender may get reconstructive surgery so that their bodies reflect more aptly who they really are. Transgenders in certain locations may also have their birth certificates amended to state their correct gender, but unfortunately, this right is not granted in all states.

Hate-Crime Legislation

The vicious anti-Gay murders of Gays and Lesbians have revealed that hate-motivated violence is still a major problem for the GLBTQ community. Laws that increase the penalty for crimes motivated by prejudice will further convey that prejudice is unacceptable, and will greater protect GLBTQ people from homophobic-based attackers. Some hate-crime laws are on the books of different states, but it has yet to be a nation-wide policy against the persecution of Gay people.

DOES YOUR STATE'S HATE-CRIME LAW INCLUDE "SEXUAL ORIENTATION"?		
Hate-Crime laws include "Sexual Orientation"	Hate-Crime laws do not include "Sexual Orientation"	NO Hate-Crime laws at all
Arizona	Alabama	Arkansas
California	Alaska	Georgia
Connecticut	Colorado	Hawaii
Delaware	Idaho	Indiana
Washington, D.C.	Maryland	Kansas
Florida	Michigan	New Mexico
Illinois	Mississippi	South Carolina
Iowa	Montana	Wyoming
Kentucky	New York	
Louisiana	North Carolina	
Maine	North Dakota	* the Texas statute refers to
Massachusetts	Ohio	victims selected "because of the
Minnesota	Oklahoma	defendant's bias or prejudice
Missouri	Pennsylvania	against a person or group
Nebraska	South Dakota	
Nevada	Tennessee	**Utah statute ties penalties for
New Hampshire	Texas*	hate crimes to violation of the
New Jersey	Utah**	victim's constitutional or civil
Oregon	Virginia	rights.
Rhode Island	West Virginia	
Vermont		-Lambda Legal,
Washington		www.lambdalegal.org
Wisconsin		

Networking & Politics

Gay Pride for Everyone!

Annually, cities across the nation host Gay Pride events for GLBTQ people from all over to celebrate their identities together. Hundreds upon thousands of hot guys and girls join in putting on parades, shows, gatherings, and more. Gay Pride events are loads of fun, and they present you with the opportunity to see how many people there are who are just like you. Whether you're on the West Coast, the East Side, or the "Durty South", chances are there's a Pride event near you. Here are some places in the U.S. where you can go to celebrate your uniqueness.

Arizona Central Gay Pride
Atlanta Gay Pride
Black Gay Pride NYC
Boston Gay Pride
Boulder Gay Pride
Gay Pride Buffalo
Cape Cod Pride
Cape Town Gay Pride
Central Alabama Gay Pride
Charlotte Gay Pride
Chicago Gay Pride
Cincinnati GLBT Pride
Cleveland Gay Pride
Columbus Gay Pride
Dallas Gay Pride
Delaware Gay Pride
Greater Palm Springs Gay Pride
Houston Gay Pride
Jacksonville Gay Pride
Jersey Gay Pride
Long Beach Gay Pride
Long Island Gay Pride
Los Angeles Gay Pride
Michigan Gay Pride
Milwaukee Pride Fest
New York City Gay Pride
Nyack Gay Pride
Orange County Gay Pride
Philadelphia Gay Pride
Portland Gay Pride - Oregon
Rhode Island Gay Pride
San Antonio Gay Pride
San Diego Gay Pride
San Francisco Gay Pride
San Jose Gay Pride
Santa Cruz Gay Pride Savannah Pride
Seattle Gay Pride
South Carolina Gay Pride
Syracuse Gay Pride
Washington D.C. Black Lesbian & Gay Pride
West Virginia Gay Pride

Organizations to Know

All across America, there are many people who actively work to change the landscape of this nation to be a more tolerant place for everyone. Clubs, groups, and organizations vary in motive. Some exist to provide education about GLBTQ issues. Others work to make legal reform for laws that are more inclusive of GLBTQ people. A quantity of organizations exists to provide a place of comfort to those who have been scarred by the vindictive culture of homophobia. Each group specifically adds to the collective community of GLBTQ people fighting for change; as each group makes a significant contribution its own way. Listed are some of the most prominent national groups who take aim at empowering us as a people.

(HRC) The Human Rights Campaign

The Human Rights Campaign is the largest national GLBTQ advocacy organization with a constituency nearing 600,000 members. Their goal is to build an America where GLBTQ people are ensured of their basic equal rights, and can be open, honest, and safe at home, at work and in the community.

The HRC effectively lobbies Congress, provides campaign support to fair-minded candidates, and works to educate the public on a wide array of topics affecting GLBTQ Americans, including workplace, family, discrimination, and health issues.

The Human Rights Campaign advocates for federal legislation to end discrimination on a variety of issues, and educates elected officials and policy makers in Washington on issues of importance to the GLBT community.

Here are some of the battles currently being fought by the Human Rights Campaign:

Marriage
The national debate about whether or not same-sex couples should be allowed to receive a marriage license has elevated after Ontario and British Columbia legalized same-sex marriage and the Supreme Court declared sodomy laws unconstitutional.

Workplace Discrimination
Gay, lesbian, and bisexual employees can be fired on the basis of their sexual orientation in 34 states. Transgender employees can be fired on the basis of their gender identity and expression in 44 states.

Immigration
Current U.S. immigration law does not allow lesbian and Gay citizens or permanent residents to petition for their same-sex partners to immigrate.

Privacy Issues
On June 26, 2003, the U.S. Supreme Court handed down its decision in *Lawrence v. Texas*. The Court overturned Texas' sodomy law as a violation of privacy rights under the due process clause of the 14th Amendment.

Health
HRC's health work has historically been focused on issues surrounding the HIV/AIDS pandemic, but has broadened to encompass a wide variety of health issues that impact the LGBT community.

Hate Crimes
Anti-Gay hate crimes are underreported, increasing, and state laws are inadequate. The federal hate crimes bill does not include hate crimes based on sexual orientation, gender, or disability.

Transgender Issues
There is a lack of public education and understanding of issues faced by the transgender community, in addition to the discrimination against the entire GLBT community.

Military
Under the U.S. military's "don't ask, don't tell, don't pursue, don't harass" policy, Gay, lesbian and bisexual service members are prohibited from serving openly. Current military regulations also medically disqualify transsexual men and women from service.

(ACLU) American Civil Liberties Union

The American Civil Liberties Union is a nonprofit, nonpartisan, membership organization devoted to protecting the basic civil liberties of all Americans, and extending them to groups that have traditionally been denied their basic civil rights.

The American Civil Liberties Union fights for equal treatment, fairness, privacy, freedom of speech, and freedom to practice religion. The struggle for legal equality for lesbians and Gay men rests on several fundamental constitutional principles. The ACLU supports every person's right to make personal decisions - without government interference - about religion, abortion, marriage, and other family and lifestyle matters.

Lambda Legal Defense

Lambda Legal is a national organization committed to achieving full recognition of the civil rights of Lesbians, Gay men, bisexuals, transgender people and those with HIV through impact litigation, education, and public policy work.

Lambda Legal carries out its legal work principally through test cases selected for the likelihood of their success in establishing positive legal precedents that will affect lesbians, Gay men, Bisexuals, the Transgendered, and people with HIV or AIDS. Lambda Legal offices exist in cities nationwide, including New York, Los Angeles, Chicago, Atlanta, and Dallas.

Lambda Legal pursues litigation in all parts of the country, in every area of the law that affects the GLBTQ community and/or people with HIV. This includes discrimination in employment, housing, public accommodations, and the military; HIV/AIDS-related discrimination and public policy issues; parenting and relationship issues; equal marriage rights; equal employment and domestic partnership benefits; "sodomy" law challenges; immigration issues; anti-Gay initiatives; and free speech and equal protection rights.

National Black Justice Coalition

The National Black Justice Coalition is a civil rights organization of Black Lesbian, Gay, Bisexual and Transgender people and our allies dedicated to fostering equality by fighting racism and homophobia. The NBJC advocates for social justice by educating and mobilizing opinion leaders, including elected officials, clergy, and media, with a focus on Black communities.

(GLAAD) The Gay & Lesbian Alliance Against Defamation

The Gay & Lesbian Alliance Against Defamation is dedicated to promoting and ensuring fair, accurate and inclusive representation of people and events in the media as a means of eliminating homophobia and discrimination based on gender identity and sexual orientation.

(GLSEN) The Gay, Lesbian and Straight Education Network

The Gay, Lesbian and Straight Education Network strives to assure that each member of every school community is valued and respected regardless of sexual orientation or gender identity/expression. GLSEN is the leading national education organization focused on ensuring safe schools for ALL students.

(PFLAG) Parents, Families & Friends of Lesbians & Gays

PFLAG is a national support, education and advocacy organization for Gay, Lesbian, Bisexual and Transgendered people, their families, friends, and allies.

PFLAG supports the GLBTQ community through local PFLAG chapter help-lines, and support group meetings, and locally and nationally produced resources. PFLAG educates families and provides public education on sexual orientation, gender identity and GLBTQ issues. PFLAG chapters educate their communities through a variety of local projects, and nationally PFLAG continues to provide fair and accurate information about GLBTQ people and their loved ones. PFLAG also advocates for equal rights for Gay, Lesbian, Bisexual and Transgendered people. Locally, PFLAG activists work for change in their communities. Nationally, PFLAG staff and volunteer leaders lobby for fairness and acceptance.

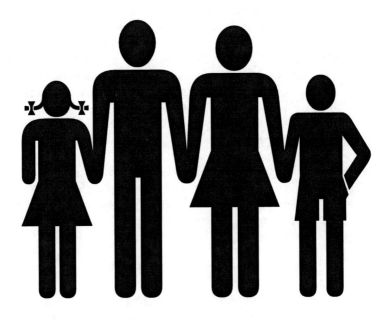

DIRECTORY
OF
BLACK GAY
ORGANIZATIONS

ALABAMA

Lesbians and Gays of Color, 2825 Highland Ave. #7, Birmingham 35205, 205-251-1232.

ARKANSAS

Rapps for Human Rights, Box 165235, Little Rock 72216, 501-224-5284 or 501-661-0719.

CALIFORNIA

At the Beach, Box 480439, Los Angeles 90048, 213-969-1619.

Bisexuals of Color Caucus, 584 Castro St. #422, San Francisco 94114, 415-821-3534.

Black Gay Men's Coalition for Human Rights, 9001 Keith Ave., W. Hollywood 90069, 213-274-3398.

Black Men's Xchange, 105 S. Locust St., Inglewood 90308-1812, 310-419-1961

Black, Single and Fine, 3717 S. La Brea Ave. #278, Los Angeles 90016, 213-683-3934.

Black Gay Men's Rap Group, 5149 W. Jefferson Blvd., Los Angeles 90016, 213-936-4948, 213-936-4973 (fax).

Brother-2-Brother/Los Angeles, 1219 S. La Brea Ave., Los Angeles 90019, 213-964-7828, 213-964-7820, 213-964-7830 (fax).

Calafia, 528 Merritt Ave. #102, Oakland 94610, 510-465-6294.

Gay and Lesbian African Americans, Box 813, Sacramento 95812-0813, 916-635-3229.

Gentlemen Concerned, Box 691157, Los Angeles 90069, 310-274-3398.

Lesbians and Gays of African Descent for Democratic Action, Box 584 Castro St. #130, San Francisco 94114, 415-957-3613.

Men of All Colors Together/San Francisco Bay Area, 973 Market St. #600, San Francisco 94103, 415-675-0201, mactsfba@aol.com

Men of All Colors Together/Los Angeles, 7985 Santa Monica Blvd. #109-136, W. Hollywood 90046, 213-664-4716.

Multicultural Prevention Resource Center, 2186 Geary Blvd. #311, San Francisco 94115-3457, 415-861-2142.

National Body of the Black Men's Xchange, Box 8216, Inglewood 90308-8216,

COLORADO

African-American Gay Men's Group, Gay and Lesbian Community Center of Colorado, 1245 E. Colfax #319, Denver 80218, 303-831-6268.

International African Pride & Power Organization, 9249 S. Broadway, #200-423, Highlands Ranch, 80129, 303799-0506, allthewords@aol.com.

CONNECTICUT

Mosaic, 25 Van Zan St., E. Norwalk 06855, 203-853-0600.

DISTRICT OF COLUMBIA

Black Lesbian and Gay Pride, Box 77071, Washington 20013, 202-667-8188, 800- 94-BLGPD, blkpridedc@aol.com

Black and White Men Together/DC, Box 73111, Washington 20056-3111, 202-452-9173.

D.C. Coalition of Black Lesbians and Gay Men, Box 77145, Washington 20013-8145.

Exquisite Gentlemen Fraternity, Box 75009, Washington 20013-0009, www.geocities.com/WestHollywood/Heights/1988

National Association of Black and White Men Together, 1747 Connecticut Ave., N.W., Washington 20009-1142, 800-NA4-BWMT, 202-462-3599, 202-462-3690 (fax)

DELAWARE

Delaware Lesbians and Gays, 601 Delaware Ave., 5th Fl., Wilmington 19801.

FLORIDA

Bay Area Men of All Colors Together/Tampa, 1222 S. al Mabry #918, Tampa 33629-5009, 813-831-7454.

BGM United Voices, Box 370622, Miami 33137.

Black and White Men Together/Tallahassee/Big Bend, Box 926, Tallahassee 32302-0926, 904-681-9299.

Black and White Men Together/South Florida, Box 5212, Hollywood 33083-5212, 954-463-4528, 954-962-5317 (fax) sfbwmt@aol.com.

Family, Box 552552, Miami 33055, 305-769-3500.

Gay Men of Color Discussion Group, Miami, 305-672-0865.

GEORGIA

Adodi Muse, Box 92097, Atlanta 30314, adodimuse1@aol.com

Black and White Men Together/Atlanta, Box 1334, Atlanta 30301-1334, 404-892-BWMT.

Boyz of Distinction, Box 78091, Atlanta 30531.

ILLINOIS

Brother II Brother, 5401 S. Wentworth, Chicago 60609, 773-288-6900, 773-268-3020 (fax).

Chicago Black Lesbians and Gays, 5828 N. Winthrop Ave., Chicago 60660-3512, 773-275-8669, 773-871-2117.

Group Dialogue, 7820 S. Lowe Ave., Chicago 60620-1829, 773-224-5142.

Men of All Colors Together/Chicago, Box 408922, Chicago 60640-8922, 312-409-6916.

Onyx, 1340 W. Irving Park Rd. #188, Chicago 60613.

KENTUCKY

Black and White Men Together/Louisville, Box 4652, Louisville 40204, 502-366-2949.

LOUISIANA

Men of Color, Box 57694, New Orleans 70157, 504-482-5341, moc482@aol.com

Men of All Colors Together/New Orleans, Box 52801, New Orleans 70152-2801.

De Colores, 215 Essex St., Holyoke 01040, 413-533-1148, 413-584-7280.

Men of All Colors Together/Boston, 398 Columbus Ave. #255, Boston 02116.

Umoja, 43 Dale St. #3, Roxbury 02119.

MARYLAND

People of All Colors Together/Baltimore, Box 33186, Baltimore 21218, 410-366-9565.

Umoja, Box 41401, Baltimore 21203-6401, 800-99-UMOJA.

MICHIGAN

All Us, 3117 Michigan Union, Ann Arbor 48104, 313-764-0158, all.us@umich.edu

Black and White Men Together/Detroit, Box 441562, Detroit 48244-1562, 810- 695-2383, bwmtdet@sprynet.com

Detroit Black Gay Pride, Box 3025, Detroit 48231, 313-438-0704.

James Baldwin-Pat Parker Society, Box 2808, Detroit 48226.

Men of Color Motivational Group, 3028 E. Grand Blvd., Detroit 48202.

People of All Colors Together/Black and White Men Together/Men of All Colors Together, Box 2133, Battle Creek 49016-2133, 616-969-5330.

MISSOURI

Kaleidoscope, Box 411174, Kansas City 64141.

Men of All Colors Together/Kansas City, Box 412432, Kansas City 64141, 816- 531- 5579, kc4mact@aol.com

People of All Colors Together/St. Louis, Box 775402, St. Louis 63177-5402, 314-995- 4683.

NORTH CAROLINA

Black and White Men Together/Charlotte, Box 29061, Charlotte 29229-9061, 704-375- 6477.

Black Men United, Box 71283, Durham 27722-1283, 919-479-0136, 919-477-5542 (fax), jerryvhm@ix.netcom.com

Brothers of Umoja, Box 288, Charlotte 28204, 704-559-4106, 704-537-7585 (fax).

Men of All Colors Together/Triangle, Box 3411, Durham 27702-3411.

Men of All Colors Together/Greensboro-Triad, Box 14327, Greensboro 27415, 910-274- 9259.

Triangle Coalition of Black Lesbians and Gays, BPW Club Rd., #A-11, Carrboro 27510, 919-933-6548.

NEW JERSEY

People of All Colors Rap Group, Morristown Unitarian Fellowship, 21 Normandy Heights Rd., Morristown 07111.

Society of Homosexuals of African Descent of Essex and Southward, 4 Little St., Newark 07107, 201-485-5689.

NEW YORK

Adodi/New York, 543 W. 43rd St. #8045, New York 10036, 718-712-0014.

African Ancestral Lesbians United for Societal Change, 208 W. 13th St., New York 10011, 212-620-7310.

Audre Lorde Project, 85 S. Oxford St., 3rd Fl., Brooklyn 11217, 718-596-0342, 718-596-1328 (fax), 718-670-3244 (events).

Aya Institute, 85 S. Oxford St., Brooklyn 11212, 718-596-0342 x23, 718-596- 1328 (fax), aya21blkyn@aol.com

Brotherhood of the Gentlemen, Box 1411, New York 10185, 212-802-8225.

Caribbean-Identified Lesbian and Gay Alliance, 81-12 Roosevelt Ave. #702, Jackson Heights 11372-6746, 718-670-7399.

Gay African Americans of Westchester, 508 Warburton Ave. #2, Yonkers 10701-1832, 914-376-0727.

Gay Men of African Descent, 133 W. 4th St., New York 10012, 212-420-0773, 212-982-1182 (fax).

Gay Men of the Bronx, Box 511, Bronx 10451, 718-378-3497.

International Lesbian and Gay People of Color Human Rights Task Force, 11-15 FDR Dr. #7E, New York 10009, 212-254-5506.

Lavender Light: The Black and People of All Colors Lesbian and Gay Gospel Choir, 70A Greenwich Ave. #315, New York 10011, 212-714-7072, mcjellyrol@aol.com

Lesbian and Gay People of Color Steering Committee, 210 Riverside Dr. #11H, New York 10025, 212-222-9794.

Men of All Colors Together/New York, Box 907, New York 10023, 212-330-7678.

People of Color Queers of Multi-Racial and Ethnic Descent, Box 7045, New York 10116-7045, 212-969-8724, 718-857-4723.

Sisters and Brothers in the Life, 332 Hudson Ave., Albany 12207.

Wazobia, Box 8264, New York 10116-8264.

OHIO

Black and White Men Together/Youngstown, Box 1131, Youngstown 44501-1131.

Black and White Men Together/Cleveland, Box 5144, Cleveland 44101-0144.

Cleveland Black Pride, Box 602093, Cleveland 44102, 216-556-4740

People of Color, Columbus, 614-299-7764.

People of All Colors Together/Cincinnati, Box 140856, Cincinnati 45250-0856, 513-395-PACT, pactcincy@aol.com

PENNSYLVANIA

Adodi, Box 59559, Philadelphia 19102, 215-747-7839.

Colours, 1108 Locust St., 1st Fl., Philadelphia 19107, 215-629-1852, 215-629- 1856 (fax), colours@critpath.org

Men of All Colors Together/Philadelphia, Box 42257, Philadelphia 19101-2257, 610-277-6595 (also fax).

People of All Colors United/Pittsburgh, Box 101430, Pittsburgh 15237, 412-782-0635.

Unity, 1207 Chestnut St. #209, Philadelphia 19107, 215-851-1876, 215-851- 1912, 215-851-1878 (fax).

TENNESSEE

Black Gay and Lesbian Alliance for Dignity, 1579 Humber St., Memphis 38106, 901-948-2345.

Black and White Men Together/Memphis, Box 42157, Memphis 38174-2157, 901-323-7451, 901-276-0168, nutrlguy@aol.com

TEXAS

African American Lesbian and Gay Alliance, Box 130818, Houston 77219, 713- 526-9062, aalga@aol.com

Ebony Connection, 1643 E. 2nd St., Austin 78702, 512-926-3786.

Men of All Colors Together/Dallas, Box 190611, Dallas 75219.

Men of All Colors Together/South Central Texas, 433 W. Rosewood #1, San Antonio 78212-2241, 210-736-3948, magijay@aol.com

WASHINGTON

Brother to Brother, 1200 S. Jackson #25, Seattle 98144, 206-528-2028, 206-322-7061.

Gay/Lesbian/Bisexual Youth of Color Discussion Group, 4620 S. Findlay, Seattle 98136, 206-632-0500.

Men of All Colors and Cultures Together/Seattle, 1202 E. Pike St. #936, Seattle 98122-3918.

WISCONSIN

Men of All Colors Together/Milwaukee, Box 93127, Milwaukee 53203.

Ujima, 1442 N. Farwell St. #602, Milwaukee 53202, 414-272-3009.

!Crisis!

<u>**Depression**</u>

I will be the first to tell you, being a Black Gay male coming of age can be tough. At times, it can feel like the world is against you, problems just keep coming your way, and it seems as if no one cares. Periods of sadness and occasional feelings of helplessness are understandable - in fact - expected for every teenager. However, when one finds that this mood of melancholy limits his ability to function normally, depression may be the cause. Depression in teenagers is characterized by a persistent sad mood, anger, feelings of hopelessness or the inability to feel pleasure or happiness for an extended period of time – be it for weeks, months or even years.

Determining if you are experiencing depression may be difficult because the symptoms of adolescent depression are a normal part of the difficulties of life for everyone – especially adolescents. However, signs that you or someone you know may be depressed are:

- changes in eating and sleeping habits (eating and sleeping too much or too little)
- missing school or poor school performance
- withdrawing from friends and activities
- indecision, lack of concentration, or forgetfulness
- feelings of worthlessness or guilt
- overreaction to criticism
- feeling that nothing is worth the effort
- frequent health complaints when no physical ailment exists
- anger, rage, anxiety
- lack of enthusiasm and motivation
- drug/alcohol abuse, thoughts of death or suicide

Symptoms such as insomnia, panic attacks, delusions, or hallucinations can indicate extreme depression, with particular risk for suicide.

Depression takes effect on the behaviors and attitudes of the person who is experiencing it. Changes in how someone acts can be correlated to feelings of depression. Depressed teens often use drugs and/or alcohol in an attempt to self-medicate their symptoms. Depression can intensify one's low self-esteem. Eating disorders (anorexia, bulimia, binge eating, or yo-yo dieting) are often signs of unrecognized depression. Be especially aware of self-mutilation. Cutting, burning, head banging, or other kinds of self-mutilation are almost always associated with depression. Also, depression in teenagers may appear as agitation, aggression, or high risk behaviors rather than (or in addition to) gloominess. And most noteworthy, teens who are seriously depressed often think, speak, or make "attention-getting" attempts at suicide, WHICH SHOULD BE TAKEN SERIOUSLY!

Depression is a serious and stubborn mental and physical disability. It involves a fundamental impairment in areas of the brain that support motivation, energy, and hope.

Because of the complexity of depression, recovery may involve more than one kind of intervention. The first step to getting appropriate treatment is a physical examination by a doctor. Certain medications as well as some medical conditions, such as a viral infection, can cause the same symptoms as depression. A physician should rule out these other possibilities through examination, interview, and lab tests. If a physical cause for the depression is ruled out, a social and emotional evaluation should be done by a therapist or counselor.

A good diagnostic evaluation will include a complete history of symptoms and possible causes. The following are some of the questions that may be asked:

- When did the symptoms start?
- Was there an event or series of events that may have triggered this?
- How long have the symptoms lasted?
- How severe are the symptoms?
- Has the patient had these symptoms before?
- Did the patient receive treatment?
- What treatment was given?
- Does the patient use alcohol? Drugs?
- Have other family members had a depressive illness?
- What kind of social support does the patient have in place?
- What lifestyle factors (work, diet, exercise, recreation, etc.) may be connected?
- Has the patient had thoughts about death or suicide?

Depressed people can help themselves, but they need to know that recovery involves a series of hard choices over a long period of time – five months, on average. One must *choose* to get out of bed, *choose* to eat breakfast, *choose* to shift attention from negative thoughts to at least neutral ones, and *choose* to help themselves. In making lifestyle changes, start with the easiest, most do-able changes, and go from there.
Useful strategies to help you overcome depression:

- Set attainable goals.
- Assume a reasonable amount of responsibility.
- Break large tasks into small ones, set some priorities, and do what you can when you can.
- Try to spend time with other people, and confide in someone. Spending time with people is usually better than being alone and secretive.
- Engage in activities that may make you feel better.
- Engage in stimulating exercise.
- Participate in social events, including movies, a ballgame, or other activities.
- Expect your mood to improve gradually, not immediately. Feeling better takes time.
- Postpone important decisions until the depression has lifted. Before deciding to make a major transition like changing jobs, or getting married or divorced, discuss it with others who know you well and have a more objective view of your situation.
- Remember: positive thinking will replace the negative thoughts that are part of the depression. They will disappear as your depression responds to treatment.
- Let your family and friends help you.

Suicide

A national study found that Gay and Bisexual teens are more than twice as likely to be suicidal as their straight counterparts. Fifteen percent of kids with an attraction toward the same sex had considered or attempted suicide, compared to seven percent of the rest. Gay teens are at higher risk of suicide usually because they feel misunderstood or rejected by their families.

Talking about one's feelings to a trusted person can help a suicidal teen significantly. Share your worries with someone who will listen and who cares, especially a trained professional who can guide you to feeling better. Reach out and talk to friends, parents, or teachers. If you are stressed out by exams, talk to your teacher or school counselor. Avoid hanging out with people who use drugs or alcohol to cope with feelings. Remember you are not alone.

Depression is a common problem and usually a passing state. Even though it feels like it will never lift, depression almost always does come and go on its own – and with proper intervention, it can be controlled, greatly reduced, or overcome. You might need medication to temporarily help you while you sort out your feelings. Be sure your parents look into this before deciding, as some antidepressants used with adults can actually make teens feel worse. Above all, do not do anything that can cause permanent damage or death. Suicide is a permanent solution to a temporary problem.

If you have a depressed friend, especially one who talks about suicide or is giving things away, DO NOT consider it a betrayal to tell a responsible adult. Depression depletes energy and clouds judgment, and your friend may do something that can never be repaired if help is not received. Even if you promised not to tell, your friend needs your help, and you would rather have a friend who is temporarily angry at you than one who is no longer alive.

If you think someone may be suicidal:

Trust your instincts. The person may or may not show some of the signs above. Even if you're not sure, don't be afraid about asking the person if he or she is feeling suicidal. You won't be putting ideas into someone's head, but instead are bringing out a topic that has most likely been thought of already.

Notice the level of action. Does the person have a plan for suicide? Having a plan means the person is that much more serious about intending suicide. Does he or she have means to carry out the plan? Talking about pills or guns is much more serious if the person actually has them in possession, or has access to them. Does the person have a history of prior suicide attempts? The more times a person has already attempted suicide, the greater the risk of succeeding.

Get involved. Some people worry that if they "butt in," the person might be angry with them. While this might occur, you would undoubtedly rather have someone alive and angry at you than wonder later if your involvement might have prevented a death. If someone is feeling suicidal, the most important thing you can provide is support and unconditional acceptance.

- Recognize that he/she is in almost unbearable pain. Listen to the person, and accept feelings without judging or discounting them.
- Tell the person you care about him/her, and want to help make a plan to feel better.
- Call a crisis line yourself to get information and suggestions – counselors can give you some tips as well as some starting resources for developing a plan to get the person the care needed. This might be developing a support system, counseling, or getting in touch with the treatment team if s/he has a mental illness.
- If you can't develop a plan and a suicide attempt seems to be imminent, **don't wait – get help**. You could be saving a life. Call a local crisis center or dial 911 if it is an emergency. Do not leave the person alone.
-

Be sure to **take care of yourself** as well. It can be very scary when someone close to you is contemplating suicide, and can be difficult to talk about. Find someone that you trust, whether a friend, other family member, or counselor, to share your feelings.

Child Abuse

Abuse of minors takes many forms. The Black Gay youth whose father is enraged at his son's homosexuality may take severe action. The relative who learns of his Gay nephew's sexuality may decide to try to "teach a lesson" to the young boy. The mother who feels her son will never change, may give up hope and avert her attention away from the child's needs. Child abusers inflict physical, sexual, and emotional trauma on defenseless adolescents every day. The scars can be deep and long-lasting, and the more subtle forms of child abuse such as neglect and emotional abuse can be just as traumatizing as violent physical abuse.

Child abuse consists of any act or failure to act that endangers a child's physical or emotional health and development. A person caring for a child is abusive if he or she fails to nurture the child, physically injures the child, or relates sexually to the child. The four major types of child abuse are (1) physical, (2) sexual, (3) emotional, and (4) neglect.

PHYSICAL

Physical abuse is any non-accidental physical injury to a child. Even if the parent or caretaker who inflicts the injury might not have intended to hurt the child, the injury is not considered an accident if the caretaker's actions were intentional. This injury may be the result of any assault on a child's body, such as:
- beating, whipping, paddling, punching, slapping, or hitting
- pushing, shoving, shaking, kicking or throwing
- pinching, biting, choking, or hair-pulling
- burning with cigarettes, scalding water, or other hot objects.
- severe physical punishment that is inappropriate to child's age.

SEXUAL

Sexual abusers can be parents, siblings, or other relatives; childcare professionals; clergy, teachers, or athletic coaches; neighbors or friends; or strangers. Sexual abuse of a child is any sexual act between an adult and a child. This includes:

- fondling, touching, or kissing a child's genitals
- making the child fondle the adult's genitals
- penetration, intercourse, incest, rape, oral sex or sodomy
- exposing the child to adult sexuality in other forms (showing sex organs to a child, forced observation of sexual acts, showing pornographic material, telling "dirty" stories, group sex including a child)
- other privacy violations (forcing the child to undress, spying on a child in the bathroom or bedroom)
- sexual exploitation
- enticing children to pornographic sites or material on the Internet
- luring children through the Internet to meet for sexual liaisons
- exposing children to pornographic movies or magazines
- child prostitution
- using a child in the production of pornography, such as a film or magazine

EMOTIONAL

Emotional abuse is any attitude, behavior, or failure to act on the part of the caregiver that interferes with a child's mental health or social development.
Other names for emotional abuse are:
- verbal abuse
- mental abuse
- psychological maltreatment or abuse

Emotional abuse can range from a simple verbal insult to an extreme form of punishment. The following are examples of emotional abuse:
- ignoring, withdrawal of attention, or rejection
- lack of physical affection such as hugs
- lack of praise, positive reinforcement, or saying "I love you"
- yelling or screaming
- threatening or frightening
- negative comparisons to others
- belittling; telling the child he or she is "no good," "worthless," "bad," or "a mistake"
- using derogatory terms to describe the child, name-calling
- shaming or humiliating
- habitual scapegoating or blaming
- using extreme or bizarre forms of punishment, such as confinement to a closet or dark room, tying to a chair for long periods of time, or terrorizing a child
- parental child abduction

NEGLECT

Neglect is a failure to provide for the child's basic needs. The types of neglect are physical, educational, and emotional. **Physical neglect** is not providing for a child's physical needs, including inadequate provision of food, housing, or clothing appropriate for season or weather; lack of supervision; expulsion from the home or refusal to allow a runaway to return home; abandonment; denial or delay of medical care; and inadequate hygiene.

Educational neglect is the failure to enroll a child of mandatory school age in school or to provide necessary special education. This includes allowing excessive truancies from school.

Emotional (psychological) neglect is a lack of emotional support and love, such as:
- not attending to the child's needs, including need for affection
- failure to provide necessary psychological care
- domestic violence in the child's presence, such as spousal or partner abuse
- drug and alcohol abuse in the presence of the child, or allowing the child to participate in drug and alcohol use

Some signs of physical abuse
- Unexplained burns, cuts, bruises, or welts in the shape of an object
- Bite marks
- Anti-social behavior
- Problems in school
- Fear of adults
- Drug or alcohol abuse
- Self-destructive or suicidal behavior
- Depression or poor self-image

Some signs of emotional abuse
- Apathy
- Depression
- Hostility
- Lack of concentration
- Eating disorders

Some signs of sexual abuse
- Inappropriate interest in or knowledge of sexual acts
- Seductiveness
- Avoidance of things related to sexuality, or rejection of own genitals or bodies
- Nightmares and bed wetting
- Drastic changes in appetite
- Overcompliance or excessive aggression
- Fear of a particular person or family member
- Withdrawal, secretiveness, or depression
- Suicidal behavior
- Eating disorders
- Self-injury

Sometimes there are no obvious physical signs of sexual abuse, and a physician must examine the child to confirm the abuse.

Some signs of neglect
- Unsuitable clothing for weather
- Being dirty or unbathed
- Extreme hunger
- Apparent lack of supervision

Getting Help

Call the National Child Abuse Hotline:
1-800-4-A-CHILD (1-800-422-4453)

Some kids are afraid to report the abuse because they fear punishment, loss of love, or family dishonor for telling a secret. The hotline will make sure you are protected from further abuse. They will help you to report the abuse to an agency that will make sure you are safe. The hotline staff members will call Child Protective Services or the police and stay on the line in a three-way call to help you talk to the agency. Even if you have told the person who is abusing you that you will keep a secret about the things you do together, it is okay to call the hotline and get help for yourself.

The hotline can help you find ongoing support from caring adults. It is not your fault that you are being abused, and you need help from other adults to protect your safety. If the abuse is within your own family, you need protection while your family learns new ways to act with each other.

Prostitution

Another problem Black Gay youth often face is sexual exploitation – either by someone else, or by themselves. Common among young transgendered youth is the activity of supporting themselves financially through sexual labor. In many cases, the youth has been cut off from any financial support from a parent or guardian, and prostitution is the only means by which they can survive. Prostitution may be a source of quick cash, but it is by far one of the most dangerous ways any young Black Gay man can make a living. It increases our risk for spreading STIs, raises the possibility of rape, abuse, and death, and it detracts from the physical, mental, and social development of the teenaged worker engaging in prostitution.

But the wrongs of prostitution are known, so instead of preaching to you about why selling yourself for money is bad, I'm going to present you with a safe and feasible alternative should you or someone you know fall into this life of lowliness and misery. Despite the large number of Black Gay male prostitutes in need of guidance, the majority of support shelters available for help cater exclusively to women. Coupled with the general population's lack of awareness of male prostitutes (or unwillingness to admit that male prostitution exists), young Black Gay sex workers are left with no hope in restoring their dignity and getting themselves off of the streets.

Nightly, Black Gay teenagers are trapped into exchanging sexual favors for sums of money, but little or no resources are available to either prevent them from starting or to help them stop. What's worse is that sexually abused young men are more likely to become themselves abusers, prostitute recruiters, or pimps – thus perpetuating the cycle of sexual degradation in the Black Gay community.

If you or someone you know has or is soliciting sex, these steps can lead to one's liberation – physically, mentally, and emotionally:

Get away. The prostitution life can seem to pull you in, even more so when you are trying to get escape it. Avoid any hazardous individuals who will try to force or forcefully persuade you back into something you don not want to do. Be firm on your stance, and resolute no matter what.

Get tested. Infections passed through sexual activity spread like wildfire, and often you never know when or from whom you contracted them. The most important thing in preserving your life is knowing if you have any STIs. Clinics are set up in most cities, often free of charge. Go to one and ask for help in assuring that your health is in good shape,

Sex plays on the mind. Repeated sex with no emotional involvement can alter your ideas on sexual activity and can cause you to react differently to different people. IF you plan on having any relationships for the rest of your life, seek counseling to discuss your psychological health in regards to sex. You may also be urged to address pass sexual abuses. This is OK. In order to restore yourself to live as a functioning member of society, your psychological health must be intact.

Be proud. Put the mistakes you have made in the past behind you and focus on the positives of your life now. Be proud that you have the strength and courage to overcome obstacles set in front of you.

The Black Gay Man's Glossary

0-9

69 – *(noun)* simultaneous fellatio, belly to belly, head to tail. Also applies to a similar position for heterosexual couples.

A

age of consent - *(noun)* the lowest age at which sex is legally permissible. Often the age differs for male/male, female/female and male/female relationships. In the USA, the age of consent varies state by state from 16 to 18.

aggressive – *(adjective)* adjective for having sex vigorously, even violently.

AIDS - *(noun)* Acquired Immune Deficiency Syndrome. The terminal stages of HIV infection. Fatal virus.

AIDS quilt - *(noun)* quilt squares bound together to commemorate the lives of those who died of HIV/AIDS.

anal intercourse – *(noun)* the act of inserting a penis into an anus.

anal masturbation - *(noun)* masturbation that stimulates the male prostate gland on the inside front of the anus; may be done with a finger, dildo, vibrator or other object. Usually some penile stimulation is used simultaneously.

anus - *(noun)* the hole between your legs at the rear; butt hole

asexual - *(adjective)* without sexual desire or orientation.

areola - *(noun)* anatomical name for the ring of darker skin around the nipple.

auto-erotic - *(adjective)* being attracted to people who look like yourself, or being sexually attracted to yourself.

B

B & D - *(noun)* Bondage and Discipline or Bondage and Dominance. Sexual act involving the physical restraint of one or more individuals and their control by the other(s).

ball – *(noun)* (1) the huge party centered around the art of voguing; (2) a testicle; (3) to have sex with uninhibitedly (i.e., to put one's penis in an anus right up to the balls).

baller – *(noun)* one who spends lots of money and flaunts it; also a basketball player

bareback – *(verb)* to have anal sex without using a condom; abbreviated – BB

bear - *(noun)* an older large hairy man, usually with body and facial hair, but can also be bald

bi – *(adjective)* bisexual; enjoys sex with men and women.

bigot - *(noun)* someone who likes persecuting groups of people such as Gays, Blacks or Jews.

bitch – *(noun)* used two ways: (1) as a term of endearment *"That's my bitch!"* or (2) term to degrade *"Shut up, bitch!"*

bling – *(noun) adj. (to bling)*; to wear expensive jewelry fashionably.

blk – *(adjective)* abbreviation for "black".

blowjob – *(noun)* slang term for oral sex, although nothing is actually blown on during the practice.

bondage – *(noun)* the act of imposing physical restraints (i.e., gags, ropes, handcuffs) as part of sex.

bottom – *(noun)* the sexual partner who is the recipient of the penis during anal intercourse.

boy – *(adjective)* masculine; possessing behaviors traditionally associated with men or boys rather than women or girls; *"He looks really boy"*.

breeder – *(noun)* derogatory word referring to a heterosexual.

brotha – *(noun)* also brother; black male.

buff - *(adjective)* gym-toned.

butch – *(adjective)* having masculine qualities.

C

casual sex - *(noun)* sex without commitment or love, usually for one time only.

chubby chaser - *(noun)* someone who prefers large or overweight partners.

circumcision – *(noun)* the surgical procedure in which the flap of skin covering the infant penis is cut off as a religious or health rite. This leaves a discontinuity in coloring on the shaft of the penis. Don't confuse the edge of the glans (the mushroom like tip) with the circumcision scar. Uncut guys have a glans too, that you can see when the pull back the foreskin. A man who has undergone circumcision is **circumcised**.

clean – *(adjective)* (1) to be infection/STI free; (2) to be free from former drug use or abuse.

clocked – *(verb)* (1) when it is recognized that someone is transsexual; (2) to hit someone in the face.

closet case - *(noun)* someone who is homosexual but refuses to admit it to himself or to associate with other homosexuals.

cock – *(noun)* penis.

cock ring - *(noun)* a metal or leather ring that wraps around the base of the penis, used to maintain or increase an erection; may also serve a decorative purpose.

come out – *(verb)* the process of identifying oneself as Gay or bisexual publicly.

condom - *(noun)* a latex rubber device designed primarily to keep semen or pre-cum from getting into the vagina, anus or mouth of another.

cruising – *(verb)* the act of going out into public to look for sex.

crystal dick – *(noun)* term to describe impotence caused by taking crystal meth.

cum – *(noun)* semen.

cunt – *(adjective)* an effeminate male; (2) noun; a male who acts femininely or has feminine behaviors.

curious - *(adjective)* word used to identify ambiguity on whether on is Gay, straight, or bi, but is rather exploring all options.

cut – *(adjective)* refers to a penis that has been circumcised.

D

d/d – *(adjective)* drug and infection free; see also **clean**.

daddy - *(noun)* a man who likes a young lover to whom he plays a fatherly role. It can imply spanking or other discipline.

dick – *(noun)* penis.

dildo - *(noun)* an artificial penis to use during sex or masturbation. A dildo does not have a vibrator.

doggie style – *(adjective)* having anal sex with one partner on all fours, and the other approaching from behind.

douching - *(verb)* cleaning out the rectum with water or a cleaning agent prior to anal sex.

down low - *(adjective)* refers to men whose public identification is straight, but who have discreet sex with other men outside of their primary relationship. A person who identifies this way would be said to be "on the down low", or "on the DL".

drag queen - *(noun)* a biological male who wears female clothing, often campy, glamorous, or extreme for the stage. His internal gender identity may be male or female. His sexual preference may be for males, females, or both.

dry sex – *(verb)* to engage in heavy petting and rubbing without removal of clothes.

dyke - *(noun)* originally a derogatory term for lesbians, specifically a masculine lesbian; currently is used without negative connotation to mean a lesbian who is out and proud.

E

eat (ass) – *(verb)* to use the tongue and mouth to stimulate one's anus.

Ebonics - *(noun)* Black slang.

endowed - *(adjective)* possessing a long or thick penis.

enema – *(noun)* the act of inserting liquid into the anus.

escort – *(noun)* a prostitute, a hired person to accompany with.

exhibitionist - *(noun)* one who likes others to watch when he has sex or someone who enjoys exposing their genitals in public.

F

fag - *(noun)* derogatory term for male homosexual, short for faggot.

fag hag – *(noun)* a girl whose closest friend is a Gay man.

fellatio – *(noun)* the technical term for oral sex.

femme – *(adjective)* possessing female qualities or behavior; also the more feminine partner of a lesbian couple.

fetish - *(noun)* an object, idea, or activity that somebody is irrationally obsessed with or attached to.

fingering – *(verb)* the act of inserting one or more fingers into the anus to massage the rectum and/or prostate gland.

fluffer – *(noun)* someone whose job it is backstage to arouse strippers, actors, and dancers so that their penis will be erect for performance.

foreskin - *(noun)* a hood of skin (only on uncircumcised penises) that covers the glans to keep it sensitive.

foyne – *(adjective)* like the word "fine"; meaning beautiful, sexually appealing.

frottage - *(verb)* rubbing bodies together, perhaps with oil.

FTM - *(noun)* Female To Male. A person undergoing a change of biological gender identity from female to male. They may be at any stage of the process. The process may include taking male hormones, breast reduction, creating a penis, speech training and facial surgery. Such people internally feel male, and may be sexually attracted to either males, females or both. See also **MTF**.

fuck – *(verb)* to have sexual intercourse.

G

Gay bashing – *(verb)* the violent victimization and attack of Gay people on the basis of homophobia.

Gay marriage - *(noun)* Gay marriage is the right of two men or two women to form a legal union with the same rights and responsibilities that a man and a woman have when they marry.

Gay Pride festival – *(noun)* a festival celebrating the freedom to be Gay without harassment.

Gaydar - *(noun)* the ability of Gays to tell if others are Gay, even when they are in the closet.

GBM - *(noun)* Gay Black Male; usually used in dating ads.

get your freak on - *(verb)* to have intense sex.

glans - *(noun)* medical term for the head of the penis, the mushroom-shaped part.

GLBTQ – *(adjective)* abbreviation for Gay, Lesbian, Bisexual, Transgender and Queer or Questioning.

glory hole - *(noun)* a hole in a washroom wall through which a guy inserts his penis to receive oral or anal sex.

H

Heeyyy - *(interjection)* a greeting, usually used by more effeminate Gay males.

head – *(noun)* slang term for oral sex; as in to give *head.*

heterosexual privilege – *(noun)* the freedom of heterosexual people to conduct their lives without persecution for sexuality.

HIV – *(noun)* Human Immunodeficiency Virus; either of two strains of a retrovirus, HIV-1 or HIV-2, that destroys the immune system's helper T cells, the loss of which causes AIDS.

HIV negative (-) – *(adjective)* to not have contracted HIV.

HIV positive (+) – *(adjective)* to have been diagnosed with HIV.

homo - *(noun)* an insulting word for a homosexual person.

homophile - *(noun)* literally liking people of the same gender. Used primarily in the phrase "homophile organizations" to cover a broad spectrum of groups that help homosexuals or lobby for their rights.

homophobe - *(noun)* one who is suffering from homophobia; a bigot against homosexuality.

homophobia - *(noun)* an irrational hatred, disapproval, or fear of homosexuality, homosexual men and lesbians, and their culture.

homosexual - *(noun, adjective)* someone who is sexually attracted to members of his or her own gender.

hotty - *(noun)* a good-looking, sexy young male.

I

impotence - *(noun)* the inability of a male to perform sexual intercourse, usually because erection of the penis cannot be achieved or sustained.

inches – *(noun)* refers to how long one's penis is in standard measurement of inches.

intersexed – *(noun)* one who has physical characteristics of both genders (i.e., having both a penis and ovaries).

irrumatio - *(noun)* technical term for sex involving one partner inserting his penis between the thighs of the other and rapidly humping.

ISO - *(adjective)* In Search Of..; introductory phrase before one tells what kind of partner they are seeking; usually used in dating profiles.

J

jerking off – *(verb)* slang term for masturbation.

K

kinky – *(adjective)* characterizing inventive sex, possibly inclusive of S&M, costumes, role playing, whipped cream, etc.

L

lip-lubed - *(adjective)* lubricated from saliva.

load - *(noun)* the quantity of semen in a single ejaculation. To ejaculate is to "blow one's *load*."

lover - *(noun)* a sexual partner who, most often, one lives with.

LTR - *(noun)* Long Term Relationship; a relationship that lasts for a relatively long time and has deep emotional involvement.

M

masculine – *(adjective)* possessing behaviors traditionally associated with men or boys rather than women or girls.

Matthew Shepard – *(noun)* the victim and modern-day martyr of the most famous Gay bashing incident - the crucifixion and murder of Matthew Shepard in Laramie Wyoming on October 17, 1998.

member – *(noun)* slang term for penis.

milking - *(verb)* masturbating another male using the hands.

Mixed Orientation Relationship - *(noun)* a relationship between a straight and Gay person; usually a straight woman and Gay man.

MSM – *(noun)* a Man who has Sex with Men.

MTF - *(noun)* Male To Female. A person undergoing a change of biological gender identity from male to female. They may be at any stage of the process. The process may include taking female hormones, breast augmentation, converting the penis to a vagina, hair removal, speech training, and facial surgery. Such people internally feel female, and may be sexually attracted to either males, females or both.

N

nasty – *(adjective)* word used to describe someone who likes sex wildly.

Nature vs. nurture – *(noun)* argument on whether the cause of homosexuality comes from inborn characteristic (nature) or it is something learned from the environment (nurture).

nelly - *(adjective)* mildly derogatory word for effeminate homosexuals.

Nubian – *(adjective)* of African ancestry. Strictly speaking, it refers to people whose ancestors came from the upper Nile.

O

oreo – *(noun)* a derogatory term to label an African-American who is believed to have prescribed to "White values", (like an Oreo cookie which is black on the outside, but white values on the inside).

orgy - *(noun)* group sex involving 5 or more participants.

out – *(adjective)* openly Gay.

outing – *(verb)* the act of exposing one's previously hidden sexuality to the public.

P

packing - *(verb)* wearing padding or a soft dildo to make one's crotch look fuller.

peckerhead - *(noun)* derogatory term for a white person. Some say it means his head is like a piece of dead wood that a woodpecker would peck at. Others say it means "penis head".

pedophile – *(noun)* an adult who has sexual desire for children or who has committed the crime of sex with a child.

personals – *(noun)* classified ads online, telephone, or in newspapers to advertise oneself in hopes of finding a companion.

playa – *(noun)* one who maintains multiple sexual relationships and a grandiose image; term has a positive connotation, (unlike **slut** which has the same meaning but carries negative connotation).

POZ - *(adjective)* HIV positive, carrying the HIV/AIDS virus.

premature ejaculation – *(verb)* cuming too quickly, before you or your partner has had time to enjoy themselves.

Prince Albert - *(noun)* a metal ring worn through a piercing on the underside of the tip of the penis.

prostate - *(noun)* the gland that creates pre-cum fluids during orgasm; located inside the body approximately between the anus and the belly button.

Q

queen - *(noun)* mildly derogatory word for homosexual. Used by itself refers to a flamboyant/effeminate homosexual. Used in combination with adjectives to describe a Gay man's fetish (i.e. size queen, drag queen).

queer – *(noun)* the now politically correct term for homosexual. Once a derogatory term, Gay activists have successfully made it respectable. The term is more popular with lesbians and young homosexual men.

Questioning – *(adjective)* one who is uncertain about their sexual orientation, and has yet to define their identity; see also curious.

quickie – *(noun)* a quick sexual encounter.

R

racism – *(noun)* prejudice or animosity against people who belong to other races.

rent boy – *(noun)* a young male prostitute.

rim – *(verb)* to play with or lick the anus of another.

S

safe sex - *(noun)* sexual activity in which precautions are taken to avoid spreading sexually transmitted infections, for example, by using a condom.

santorum - *(noun)* the frothy mixture of lube and fecal matter that is sometimes the byproduct of anal sex. Named to honor US Senator Rick Santorum who told reporters in April 2003 that he hoped the United States Supreme Court would uphold anti-Gay sodomy laws and compared consensual Gay sex to incest, bigamy, adultery, and bestiality.

serodiscordant - *(noun)* a relationship where one partner is HIV+ and the other HIV-.

service - *(verb)* to provide oral sex to someone.

SGL - *(noun)* Same Gendered Loving. An Afro-centric expression used to show cultural allegiance to the African-American community and independence from mainstream Gay culture.

significant other – *(noun)* a generic term one's spouse, boyfriend, or girlfriend in a primary relationship.

skank – *(noun)* one who is sleazy, especially in a sexual way.

slave - *(noun)* someone who enjoys being told what to do during sex.

slut – *(noun)* derogatory term for an extremely promiscuous person; one who is not particularly choosy about partners.

snap queen – *(noun)* a young effeminate male with exaggerated effeminate traits who typically accentuates communication with finger snaps. From the documentary "Tongues Untied" by Marlon Riggs.

sodomy - *(noun)* the legal term for anal sex.

son - *(noun)* someone who prefers an older authoritarian partner who takes a fatherly role.

STI - *(noun)* Sexually Transmitted Infection. These include HIV, gonorrhea, syphilis, chlamydia, genital herpes, trichomoniasis, genital warts and hepatitis B. Some also include parasites such as amoebas and pinworms passed by rimming.

straight – *(adjective)* heterosexual.

T

tailhook - *(noun)* a US military sex scandal with homosexual undertones.

take it – *(verb)* the act of accepting the penis (whether orally or anally).

testicles - *(noun)* medical term for balls.

threesome - *(noun)* sex involving three people.

top – *(noun)* the partner who is penetrating during anal sex.

toys – *(noun)* utensils used for sex (i.e., dildos, vibrators, cock rings, beads, and similar sexually stimulating devices).

trade – *(noun)* an attractive, thuggish, "straight-acting" young Black male.

transsexual - *(noun)* one who identifies himself or herself as and a member of the opposite sex; the identity and urge to become the opposite gender has nothing to do with sexual preference. Transsexuals may undergo surgical and hormonal treatment to change his or her anatomical sex.

transvestite – *(noun)* a male who likes dressing in female clothing; oftentimes heterosexual men.

troll - *(noun)* a derogatory term for and ugly or older person, especially one who is persistent despite in his sexual advances despite being told "NO!"

twink - *(noun)* a cute young male. Derived from Twinkie bar; one who is golden, cream-filled and ready to be eaten.

U

uncut – *(adjective)* refers to an uncircumcised penis

V

versatile – *(noun, adjective)* the partner in anal sex who can be either the recipient or the penetrator.

Viagra - *(noun)* the brand name for sildenafil citrate, a drug used to treat impotence.

vibrator - *(noun)* a penis shaped device that vibrates. It can be inserted in the anus to stimulate the prostate gland.

voguing – *(verb)* the artistic dance created by Black Gay men encompassing of flamboyant body movements that stay in tune with the beat of the music.

W

Wassup! – *(interjection)* "What's up?"; a greeting, roughly like hello.

White privilege – *(noun)* the freedom of White people to conduct their lives without racial discrimination.

X

XXX – *(noun, adjective)* relating to pornography; rated X for adult-only content.

Y

YMSM – *(noun)* Young Men who have Sex with Men.

Z

Zebrajox -*(noun)* Black guys who like White men and White men who like Black men.

Bibliography

ACLU. "About the ACLU". <u>About the ACLU</u> 2005. Retrieved 6/12/05.
    <http://www.aclu.org/about/aboutmain.cfm >

AnalSexYes.com . "Top 5 Anal Sex Tips". <u>Anal Sex "Yes"</u>. 2005. Retrieved 6/27/05.
    <http://www.analsexyes.com/top5.shtml>

BLK Publishing Company. "Political and Social Groups". <u>Organizations</u>. 2005. Retrieved 6/2/05.
    <http://www.blk.com/resources/o-political.htm>

Brown, Aaron P. "What's In a Name?". 2003. Retrieved 6/29/05.
    <http://www.balls.houseofenigma.com/what_name.html>

Brown, Karen McCarthy. "Mimesis in the Face of Fear". March 5-6, 1998. Retrieved 6/2/05

Crime PreventionTips.org. "What To Do When You're a Crime Victim". 2004. Retrieved 5/17/05.
    <http://www.crimepreventiontips.org/what-to-do.shtml>

CrimePreventionTips.org. "Public Safety". 2004. Retrieved 6/23/05.
    <http://www.crimepreventiontips.org/public-safety>

CrimePreventionTips.org. "Traveling Safety". 2004. Retrieved 6/11/05.
    <http://www.crimepreventiontips.org/traveling-safety.shtml>

DatingServices4U.com. "Internet Dating Safety Tips" 2004. Retrieved 6/1/05.
    <http://www.datingservices4u.com/internet-dating-safety-tips.htm>

Davis, Herndon L. "Standing Up to the Black Church". <u>Black Gay and Christian: An Inspirational
    Guidebook to Daily Living</u>. 2005. Retrieved 6/10/05.
    <http://www.operationrebirth.com/herndon1.html>

De Benedictis, Tina Ph.D., Jaffe, Jaelline Ph.D., and Segal, Jeanne Ph.D "Child Abuse: Types,
    Signs, Symptoms, Causes and Help". <u>Helpguide</u>. 2005. Retrieved 6/8/05.
    <www.helpguide.org/mental/child_abuse_physical_emotional_sexual_neglect.htm>

Delaney, Mike. "Four Self-Defense Tips (Just in Case ...)". 2004. Retrieved 7/3/05.
    <http://womencentral.net/defense-tips.html>

Fairchild, Betty and Hayward, Nancy. "Gays and Religion". <u>Now That You Know: A Parent's
    Guide to Understanding Their Gay and Lesbian Children</u>. 3rd Ed. Harcourt Brace &
    Company. 1998. pgs 152-155.

GLAAD. "Our Mission". 2005. Retrieved 6/29/05.
    <http://www.glaad.org/about/mission.php>

GLSEN. "Learn More About GLSEN". 2005. Retrieved 6/29/05.
    <http://www.glsen.org/cgi-bin/iowa/all/about/index.html>

Green, Roedy. "Gay & Black Glossary". <u>Canadian Mind Products</u>. 1997-2005. Retrieved 6/15/05
    <http://mindprod.com/ggloss/ggloss.html<

History Project, "The. Black & Gay History Timeline". 2005. Retrieved 6/20/05.
<www.historyproject.org/resources/bgbw_timeline.php>

Human Rights Campaign, "The. About the Human Rights Campaign". 2005. Retrieved 6/22/05.
<www.hrc.org>

Jaffe, Jaelline Ph.D., and Segal, Jeanne Ph.D. "Depression and Suicide in Teenager". Helpguide.
2005. Retrieved 6/5/05. <http://www.helpguide.org/mental/depression_teen.htm>

Jepsen, Bob. "Drugs of Abuse". 2003. Retrieved 5/31/05
<http://www.denisonia.com/police/Drug.htm>

Lambda Legal Defense and Education Fund. Issues. 2005. Retrieved 6/21/05
<http://www.lambdalegal.org/cgi-bin/iowa/issues/index.html>

Lee, Chanel. "Homos 101: Premier Black College Is a Study in Anti-Gay Discrimination". The
Village Voice. August 3-6, 2003. Retrieved 5/12/05.
<http://www.villagevoice.com/news/0333,lee,46206,1.html>

Minerva WebWorks LLC. "How to Give a Hickey". Romance Class. 2005. Retrieved 6/16/05.
<http://www.romanceclass.com/miscr/howto/hickey.asp>

National Black Justice Coalition. "Fairness for Our Families". 2005. Retrieved 6/13/05.
<http://www.nbjcoalition.org/>

Nycum, Benjie. The XY Survival Guide. San Francisco, CA. XY Publishing. 2000

PFLAG. "Vision and Mission". About PFLAG. 2005. Retrieved 6/4/05.
<http://www.pflag.org/index.php?id=188>

Sensual Love Editors. "Kissing 101: A quick lesson in the art of kissing!". 2005. Retrieved 6/17/05.
<http://www.lovingyou.com/content/sex/content.shtml?ART=howtokiss>

Shiltz, Tom. "Strategies for Prevention and Early Intervention of Male Eating Disorders". Eating
Disorders Awareness and Prevention, Inc. 2003. Retrieved 6/3/05.
<http://www.edap.org/>

St. Blaise, Vic. "Issues for Male Sex Workers". 2005. Retrieved 6/8/05.
<http://www.bayswan.org/male.html>

SwingersPersonal.net. "Fellatio". Oral Sex. 2004. Retrieved 5/27/05.
<http://www.swingerspersonals.net/oralsex.htm>

Taver, Chuck. "African Americans in the LGBT Community". 2005. Retrieved 6/9/05.
<http://www.marshall.edu/lgbo/african_american_history_month.htm>

Trebay, Guy. "Legends of the Ball: Paris Is Still Burning". The Village Voice. Aug 13-19, 2005.
Retrieved 6/30/05. <http://www.villagevoice.com/news/0002,trebay,11690,5.html>

Wessex Gay Men's Health Forum. "Sexually Transmitted Infections: a guide for Gay and bisexual
men". 2001. Retrieved 7/3/05. <http://www.gmhp.demon.co.uk/health/STI/index.html>

About the Author

Jonathan W. Jones

"When you do the common things in life in an uncommon way, you will command the attention of the world."

Jonathan Jones is without a doubt one of the most promising young teenagers of our time. Evincing his capacity for leadership and his ongoing role as a civil rights activist, Jonathan has served vital positions as President of his high school sophomore class, founder of his school's Gay-Straight Alliance, and youth advocate for GLBTQ issues. Highlights of his career have been becoming the President of the Rutgers Newark Gay And Lesbian Alliance in his Freshman year, and giving an address at the Sakia Gunn Memorial Rally in 2005. A young man who has accomplished much, Jonathan knows that success is never a destination – it is a journey forever.

Acknowledgements

This book would not be possible without the many people who encouraged me along the way, and the great many who helped me become a Black Gay youth who has survived. To the following, I acknowledge your contribution to what I am today, and what I have yet to become:

My mother, Sylvia, who without her, none of this would at all be possible.

Jason, my brother, who played the role of friend and counselor in our single-parent home.

My aunts – Carol, Beverly, Valerie, and their mother (my grandmother) who are all living testaments of what it means to be a strong Black female.

My cousins TJ. Kim, Matthew, Michael, and Donte, by my side at times, and at my throat at others.

My good friend Antwan Brown, who has always showed me the ropes to life.

To the great friends I had in High School – the divas – Shamar Green, Michael Swain, Terrell, Tyrell, Jesse Spann, Michael Seawright, Dave Robeson, Sequine, and the rest of the crew.

Mrs. Simone P. who supported students trying to make a change.

Al Cunningham, a great mentor who introduced me to the fight for social justice; I owe you a lot.

Revered LaDana Clark, who fought for me, my life, and my innocence during tough times.

Dean James Credle, a prime example of a powerful Black Gay man, who showed me more I could do.

Eddie Santiago Beck, brilliant man, who instilled in me "Where I am happiest is sword drawn, charging into battle!"

The boys and counselors of Newark's Project Wow Program, who took me in and made me feel like a brother.

Timothy B. Alston, a good man and even greater friend.

Emily Conger, who even in the brief time we knew each other, amazed me with her philosophies.

My Chemistry teacher, Dr. Watson, who told me "Wherever you are, BE there."

And the people reading this book, who actually look to understand the young Black Gay man, and work towards change.